100
TRIPS

PLACES TO DRIVE IN THE
UPPER MIDWEST

by Ben Kern

Dillon Press, Minneapolis, Minnesota 55415

©1969, 1979 by Dillon Press, Inc. All rights reserved
Second edition 1979

Dillon Press, Inc., 500 South Third Street
Minneapolis, Minnesota 55415

Printed in the United States of America

Library of Congress Cataloging in Publication Data

Kern, Ben.
  100 trips.

  1. Middle West—Description and travel—Guide—books.
I. Title.
F355.K47   1979   917.7'04'3   78-12839
ISBN 0-87518-170-8

To my wife, Julia

Grateful acknowledgement is made to the Minneapolis Tribune *and its "Your Weekend" column, in which much of the material in this book first appeared.*

TABLE OF CONTENTS

Introduction

TWENTY YEARS HAVE PASSED since my wife Julia and I began rambling around the upper Midwest, seeking things of interest to the casual traveler. Our memoirs would probably fill an encyclopedia.

To help you be selective, I offer herein a revised edition of *100 Trips* with 17 substitutions occasioned by changing conditions. If it gives you the urge to branch out here and there on your own, so much the better.

I recommend the small print names on your map, like Rollingstone, just west of the Mississippi in Winona County. It not only gathers moss, but Helen Hendricks paints pictures there, among the charming hills that were settled in the early days by Luxembourgians.

Homer, Minn., is a little hillside place on the Mississippi River bluffs on Hwy. 61 south of Winona. The town has gone history-mad, spurred by the presence of the Bunnell House, where Willard and Matilda Bunnell raised eight children. Willard named Homer after Homer, N.Y., his birthplace. The house, maintained by the Winona County Historical Society, is charming.

Schroeder is on Lake Superior's North Shore. Its waterfalls are treacherous, but its victuals are good—in a plain, little, home-cooking restaurant.

Dalbo, northeast of Elk River, is a crossroads where the postmaster handles mail for 75 local people and 500 more scattered over the surrounding farmland. Two of them, Sheri and Dale Deibert, have fashioned a fine brand of living inside a victim of school consolidation— a belfry-topped country schoolhouse.

An old habitat of yesteryear is a town called Money Creek. You'll find it in Houston County, 17 miles south of Winona. It's in a valley where the soil is rich and the buildings few. There's an old stone church with a stained-glass window. I found a garage and filling station, Ledebuhr's.

Mrs. Paul Ledebuhr told me her grandmother spent her girlhood in this valley. "We slid on these hills," she said. "And my brother skated on every pond he could find. There's no millpond any more. The dam went out."

There's a story that some pioneers camped by the creek. One lost his money. They couldn't find it, so they called it "Money Creek." There's another creek called "Money" twenty-three miles northwest. It's a bit confusing. Confusing or not, however, nosing around Houston and adjacent counties in southeastern Minnesota can be a pleasure any time of year.

Hackensack, N.J., was settled by the Dutch around 1640 near a village of the Hackensack Indians. It might have been someone from there who came west and settled Hackensack, Minn., 45 miles north of Brainerd on Hwy. 371.

North of town there's the Mascot A resort. It occupies a lakeshore building that was once the Mascot A headquarters, a communal organization based on fur farming earlier this century—fascinating story if you like delving.

Nowthen, Minn., a town northeast of Elk River, is named in honor of its postmaster, who had a habit of peppering his letters with the phrase "now then." Rental boats and fish are available in Twin Lakes, two miles west of town.

2

About 10 miles north at Crown, a name that commemorates the lofty top of a great oak tree, is Mabel Anderson's country store, and one mile north, then west, on Blue Lake is Edling's picnic ground. There we found rental boats, camping, a gas pump and dock, serve-yourself crystal-clear ice cubes, and concrete slab boat launching.

Cold Spring is a town in the hilly area southwest of St. Cloud. Good for camping and fishing. Years ago, a doctor acquired 1,208 acres for riding and fishing seven miles northwest of town. It later became a working ranch and campground that is still functioning under the Mexican-flavored name of El Rancho Manana.

At Cokato on Hwy. 12 in western Wright County, a banker named C. R. Peterson began saving local artifacts in the 1920s. With help from others the collection grew into what is a remarkable library-museum funded by a $170,000 bond issue and $40,000 in private bequests. It features top-notch interiors, photo enlargements, and such things as a diorama of an old-time pioneer farm carved in miniature by Carl Good, the son of Swedish immigrants. A block away is an antique photo studio, still functioning.

Fifteen miles north of Cokato stands a town named after a chorus girl, Lizzy Annandale. The settlers picked it off a poster. Today, it's the home of Minnesota Pioneer Park, an ambitious project involving a variety of pioneer buildings finished and furnished as in bygone days.

As it passes through Waterville, 50 miles southwest of Minneapolis on Hwys. 13 and 60, the Cannon River widens into a number of lakes. Waterville bills itself as "Bullhead Capital of the World."

Pepin, Wis., is across the Mississippi River and upstream from Wabasha, Minn., home of the Anderson

House restaurant. You'll miss the best part of Pepin if you don't turn off the main drag (Hwy. 35) riverward. There you'll see boats wobbling in their marina berths. Nearby in Ruth and Bill's Harbor View Bar and Cafe you might find Swedish meatballs or barbecued ribs, done for lunch the way you like them. Seven miles north on Hwy. 183, you'll find the reconstructed birthplace cabin of Laura Ingalls Wilder.

Tofte, named after a pioneer family on Lake Superior's North Shore, has an air of antiquity about its waterfront. Here the concrete remains of an old mail boat still take the buffeting of big waves. The gulls like it.

For a fee you can fish without a license any time of year in a private lake near Barnum, Minn., 35 miles south of Duluth on Hwy. 61 (or I-35).

Board-sidewalk connoisseurs will want to visit Mantorville, 14 miles west of Rochester on Hwy. 57. It's a treasury of nineteenth-century village architecture. An example is the Hubbell House with functioning dining room. The town will burn your name on the boardwalk. A tourists' map will point your way to the Mantorville Opera House, which features live drama in summer, and enough antique places and craft shops to make your head swim.

Sauk Centre, the birthplace of Sinclair Lewis, has a Palmer House hotel and restaurant. From there, to get off the beaten track, take Hwy. 71 about 20 miles north to Long Prairie.

Here some of the finest WPA (Works Projects Administration) ruins can be found. Persuade some old-timer to show you "the hatchery," also known as "Mosquito Park." You'll see some of the finest stone masonry recreational structures ever ruined. They were flooded out by the Long Prairie River.

Introduction

Just sitting and fishing off the banks of lakes and streams is popular throughout Minnesota, perhaps nowhere more so than in the lakes (George Walch, Peltier and Centerville lakes) just west of Centerville, which is just west of Hwy. 35E in southeastern Anoka County.

Then there's floating down the river on inner tubes. It's a growing sport that started on the Apple River at Somerset, Wis., and is spreading into Minnesota—on the Cannon River at Welch and the Rum River at St. Francis and at a campground called Rambling Rum downstream on the east bank.

There's no end to this. These are just a few random notes. Our journeys, too, were seldom organized—seldom even planned. Mostly they just happened, with the help of a few tips from the readers of my column and later, the first edition of this book. "I like your serendipity," one of them wrote. That was before the Serendipity Singers had come along. In fact, I had to look up the word ("finding agreeable things not sought for").

May you find other agreeable things not sought for, nor even mentioned, in these pages and find other byways of your own, yet to be chronicled.

BEN KERN

CHAPTER I   WINTER

Trip No. 1 / Snow in the Parks

EVER SINCE TOURING St. Paul's Como Park on skis as a boy I have been convinced that the most beautiful time of the year for any public park is in the middle of the winter under two feet of fresh snow.

If people ever discover this, the snowshoe makers will strike it rich.

Then of course, the fresh snow won't stay fresh very long, but during a good winter it won't matter. More snow will fall and the scenery will be self-renewing.

Part of the charm of winter park scenery, of course, is its being unpeopled. Until enjoying it really catches on, the scenery lover has a very good chance of catching it at its untracked best.

I have been so lucky so often at the game of plunging into snowy parks and finding them unpeopled that I've decided it isn't just luck. It's general ignorance.

I'll admit that there are snow-wading problems. Strolling around a park in your shirt sleeves in mid-July is easier than plodding through the drifts of March, by quite a bit, but a good pair of overshoes into which the slacks or downhills can be tucked should equip all but the aged or infirm for at least a sample excursion.

The source of the Mississippi in Itasca State Park is interesting enough amid the lollypop-licking log-walking kids of summer, but cutting through the snow in solitude amid the animal tracks, it's far, far different.

One of the most populous parks of summer probably is Interstate Park at Taylors Falls, Minn., and St. Croix Falls, Wis., across the river.

I stopped there mid-morning of a holiday, and there wasn't a track through the snow.

To prove my point about the scenery, I plodded around and took a few snapshots.

Beyond the wonderful muffled quiet of snow scenery is this side-product for the picture-taker: snow's shadowy black and white contrasts make it almost impossible to take a bad picture.

The dark volcanic rocks at Taylors Falls add to this contrast, and if you like sound effects, listen carefully and you're likely to hear the ice cracking in the river as it expands or contracts in the deep rock channel.

WINTER
Trip No. 2 / Nature's Rinks

OFTEN WHEN INSUFFICIENT snow delays our enjoying the snowy sports, we have a rather pleasant alternative —skating.

I'm referring to the natural or country kind of skating. Rink skating is all right, but you can enjoy the rinks and their sociability all winter.

On the other hand, natural ice offers one the tentative invitation of an introvert, and a change of mood may quickly cancel it. While it's open, however, it may reluctantly unfold, bit by bit, solitary and exploratory joys which you never will find on a rectangular rink.

It can be a treacherous invitation, too, and not for kids, unless a wary adult, who knows ice and its danger signs, has them well in hand. Country adults are best, as a rule.

Having done much of my boyhood skating on country lakes, swamps and ponds, I recently reacquainted myself with their special wonders. I hate to let an early winter go by without at least one treat of this kind.

I started out in my car at 10 a.m. of a sunny, crisp day. It was 7 above and the wind was northwest, about 10 miles an hour.

I was heading for some marshy lakes in the flatland west of Hugo. I never had skated them before, but I had seen enough of them in the summertime (just a glimpse from the Hugo-Anoka road) to be intrigued.

To my mind the least likely swimming lakes, the muddy, swampy ones that amble around among rushes, cattails, marsh grass and willows, make the best skating. For one thing the scenery, at least for a nonhunter, is a bit unusual.

On this day the grass in the fields was a bleached, wheaty beige which the sun heightened until nothing could have looked drier.

Everything was dry, dusty and dirty. Even the evergreens were a dirty green, because some of the fields were plowed and the dry cold wind had been whipping the dirt around. I like bleak scenery as much as I like verdant scenery. It has a mood of its own.

At Hugo I turned left off highway 61 on W. 1st Av. Four miles takes you into Centerville, where you turn right and follow the road past the Twin Lakes tavern (cafe, boats, bait, Saturday night dancing), which faces left on a neck between two lakes, and keep to your left.

Just 1.4 miles from the tavern I came to the Karch farm. I kept left or east for another 1/5 mile to a gnarled dead oak on the lakeshore, a wild tree with crazy branches pointing in all directions out of a partly peeled grey trunk. About 100 feet beyond this I found parking space.

Sitting on the tan grass by a white scrub oak about two feet above ice level, I put on my skates and stepped into a little snow margin which had accumulated on the south edge, blown across the ice by the northerly winds.

The wind was biting, but I would rather head into the wind at the start so I can have it at my back later on when I'm tired.

The only sign of life was a few tough little sparrows, but the ice seemed alive with overlapping, self-interrupting rumbles. It was freezing fast, and the cracks showed that already it was three to four inches thick. Also, it was smooth enough for good skating.

By walking tiptoe across the narrow band at the tavern I extended my radius. The swampland at the far northern end extended many times farther than it appeared from the road. What looked like the far shore was only an island.

I skated for an hour and a quarter and covered, I suppose, about eight miles. The sights and sounds were more than satisfying — the barking dogs (who never need frighten you on skates, because they can't turn sharp corners on smooth ice), the wind rustling the reeds, the ice sculpture, like polished Mexican onyx, where waves had dashed against brush and willows, the cottonwood with so many twigs it looked like a diagram of the nerves in the brain — even the rusty pile of rushes I flopped on for a rest at the far end.

One small confession: Returning tired and convinced that the ice was thick enough, I departed from my stick-close-to-shore resolution and was well past the middle of the smaller lake when a muffled boom brought my head up and about 50 yards ahead I saw water shimmering in a fresh crack which reached nearly from one shore to the other.

Needless to say, I headed for shore. Once around the new fissure, I opened my jacket and held it out so the wind could help me home.

WINTER
Trip No. 3 / Snow and Water

I BEG INDULGENCE to bring a special condition to your attention. The moment for action struck once, and it may strike again at any time.

I refer to the delayed freeze-up and the snow-and-water opportunities which it might produce — that is, opportunities for admiring unfrozen streams or lakes against snowy white backgrounds.

This, of course, is a scenery-viewing specialty.

I've heard it argued that there is too much specialization in today's world. Maybe so. Certainly a rich and full sight-seeing life is the one that reflects broad tastes in its variety, but here, at least, there is room for the best of both worlds — specialization and diversification.

Minor specialties always serve, I think, to sharpen the interest of a traveler. They give him something particular to look for.

It takes no special effort to discover these minor specialties, but it is not so easy to develop them. Social pressures are all in the other direction. For instance, I think I could develop a specialty in deserted houses of the falling-apart kind. I like their texture and their general air of crumbling decay. I have no idea why, and that's just as well, because if I had, it might spoil everything.

I have been unable to develop this specialty, because so far I have found it awkward to excuse myself from hose rolling, leaf raking, window washing and all such things. Otherwise I might by now have become known far and wide as a photographic documentarian of deserted houses. I have little to report that is encouraging. All I can say is that I'm looking for chances.

I also have some specialized interests in natural scenery, as distinguished from man-built structures. These have fared somewhat better. I have an interest in water —running, falling, still, frozen or liquid. But I can break it down further. My first subdivision is red autumn

leaves against water. They have to be growing on the shore with the water in the background.

This might sound like a cinch, but next fall try hunting for some red leaves standing next to or overhanging a lake or a river. The red leaves are to be found some distance back from the water's edge, you'll find. By the water you'll see things like birch and willows, which are okay in their way but whose leaves don't turn red.

I have another one that's a little easier — snow and water. If everything freezes over before it snows, then you're dead for that season, of course, but if it snows first — gangbusters! You have that water, which always looks twice as shiny and twice as dark as life, setting off the fresh white snow.

This year at a fairly good time I happened to hit a spot under the bridge, Minnesota side, across the St. Croix from Osceola, Wis., and other scenic spots in and around Osceola.

Osceola has its own waterfall, right in the center of town. If you watch on the river side as you drive through, you'll see an iron railing, and the falls are below that. A stairway with about 100 steps will take you down to the bottom of the ravine, if you prefer that vantage point.

The town fathers have seen to it that there is a floodlight on the falls at night.

Somerset, on the Apple River, south of Osceola on Hwy. 35, is another town in the same general area which offers unusual opportunities. The water rushes rapidly over a dam on one side of the bridge and past a power house on the other.

Still another spot is the Boomsite on the St. Croix just north of Stillwater on Hwy. 95. There are, of course, thousands of others.

WINTER

Trip No. 4 / Pine City in Winter

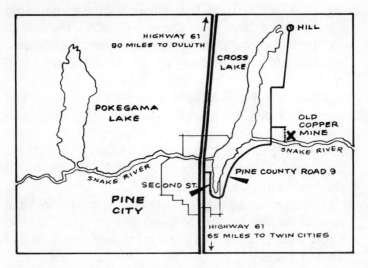

IT WAS A hot day the last time I saw Pine City and explored the two lakes (Pokegama and Cross) that connect via the Snake River running through town.

I rented an outboard at Harold Carl's Riverside Sport Shop on the Snake, right by the Hwy. 61 bridge, and took a 12-mile ride on the glaring water. The sun was blazing.

Some friends recently having returned from an ice-fishing expedition way up Hwy. 61, they aroused in me quite suddenly a desire to see what Pine City is like with the ice thick around the pilings beneath the highway bridge, against the boat docks and out into the farthest finger of Cross Lake's longest stretch.

I nosed around the river and found it just as frigidly somnolent as I had expected, and I found more than that. I found a plaque on the north side:

"A rich deposit of copper was discovered here," it said, "and a $250,000 company was formed which sank 150-foot shafts. Today the site of the old copper mine is an interesting drive for visitors and a place for the bass fisherman to try his skill."

For directions to the copper mine I was referred to "Tony" Holler, Pine County assessor. I found him in the courthouse. He drew me a map and strongly recommended that I consult with Ray Schultz, deputy county treasurer (across the hall) about ice fishing.

"I suppose your name is Anthony," I said.

"No, it's Fred."

"How come they call you Tony?"

"The story is that I didn't have any hair when I was a kid, and my father said, 'He hasn't got any more hair than Tony.' Tony was a baldheaded French butcher. So everybody called me Tony."

Ray Schultz, across the hall, told me he had caught his limit of crappies ice fishing that very morning. He advised me to run up to the north end for a look.

On the way, following Tony's map, I walked in from the road about half a mile to find a pile of slag and a rock-filled hole that once had been the copper mine shaft-opening, near the Snake. It was nothing to look at, but the hike along an abandoned road was nice, and so was the river.

Back in the car I drove up on Pine County Road 9 to the north end of Cross Lake. There was nobody in the spearhouse that I found there, and the house was no architectural wonder, but the tall stand of Norways on the bank beyond was as nice a backdrop for ice fishing as you'd want to find.

I went back and had lunch at Muriel's and Paul's, and

when I got to the Sport Shop on the Snake River, Harold
Carl was fixing something in his motel. We cut across
town to the bathing beach to look at his fish house, and
it was gone.

"Where did they take it?" he asked himself. "Oh, there it is, way over there." We drove around another corner of the lake and found Harry Commerford and his cousin, Dick Commerford, fishing in Harold's house, so far without any luck, but they had a nice fire going, and it was warm inside.

On the way back Harold said, "I'm not too busy in winter, but sometimes there are up to 50 or 60 cars on each lake. I do some fishing myself, but not a great deal."

"What do you do mostly?"

"Flatten out the pillows."

WINTER

Trip No. 5 / Winter Picnic

CAN SLOPESIDE PICKNICKING, downhill skiing, and cross-country skiing, with suitable equipment for each, all fit into a single day's trip? Yes they can, especially in late winter. On the day I tried it, February thaws had brought the ground snow into the bare-to-marginal range around the area. Machine-made snow on the slopes was holding up well, of course, and 60 miles northeast of the Twin Cities, around Dresser and St. Croix Falls, Wis., snow in the woods was adequate except on south-facing exposures.

On a bright Wednesday came word that friends of Walter J. Peterson were planning a slopeside picnic on Nisse Bakken, one of the many Trollhaugen slopes that he pioneered.

The sun was bright, the corn snow loose and easy, and Peterson available. Someone bought mustard, pickles, two dozen rolls, two dozen hotdogs, paper cups, a bag of potato chips and a jug of light table wine. There's a picnic table, grill and firewood in a northwest elbow halfway up Nisse Bakken, Trollhaugen's middle run.

Carrying the supplies, a nucleus of picnickers rode the T-bar up, skied halfway down to the picnic spot in an elbow of the run, set down the supplies, rustled up dry twigs to kindle the fire, and set out a paper cup for a kitty—$1 each, totalling $11, was sufficient in this

case. From there on it was sociability intermixed with skiing.

Peterson had said that he wanted to show me the cross-country trails in Wisconsin Interstate Park just south of St. Croix Falls (about 3 miles north of Dresser). Hence, underneath our downhill trousers we wore knee-high cross-country socks, which work just as well with the downhill boots. At 3 p.m., carrying double equipment, we drove to Interstate Park on the St. Croix riverbank and picked up trail maps at the park office. Full of enthusiasm for the trail, which he had checked out a week earlier, Peterson pronounced the ground cover adequate in the shaded woods, even though the sun was bright.

Quickly switching to cross-country togs and shoes in the parking lot nearest the trail-start, we struck out, Wally in the lead.

There were little black and white squares with arrows marking turns in the trail, nicely packed and groomed to a 3-foot width. Skis with a fishscale bottom (no wax) glided nicely in the corn snow and climbed perfectly.

On a 3-mile loop we had to make only one detour, for thaw water caught in a hollow. Part of the trail took us along the riverbank, where black open water glistened against snowy white ice.

This was no test of survival, no endurance run. It was pure pleasure—the sunlight filtering through the trees, the gleaming river. High on the rocky cliffs on the Minnesota side we could see a faraway roof rising out of the treetops, one here, another there, and still another, with windows surely commanding inspirational views.

CHAPTER II   VALLEYS

Trip No. 6 / Mankato in April

DURING APRIL, TRY A jaunt to Mankato, where the Blue Earth and Minnesota Rivers join, 78 miles southwest of Minneapolis on Hwy. 169.

When you take the exit to pass under the divided highway eastward into the middle of Mankato, you might notice some traffic. That's because you'll be entering a population center serving an estimated 130,000 shoppers, including a lot of Mankato State College students who jockey cars between the upper (new) and lower (old) campuses and in and around the various parks of Mankato, especially in the spring.

In Greater Mankato (counting North Mankato) there are four parks with picnic facilities, if you are packing a lunch, or there are restaurants.

*   *   *   *

You can't get a reasonable cross-section of this busy little city in a couple of hours, but you can pick up some interesting impressions and see some scenery.

On the upper campus of Mankato State College, handsome masonry is popping up all over the place.

On the top of the high bank, and from the edge, you can see across the valley and into the country where a lot of those 130,000 shoppers come from.

To get a high look at the immediate surroundings, I got permission to visit the room of the tallest building on the campus, Gate Center, a student dormitory.

*   *   *   *

One of the nicest brick textures I've seen in a long time graces the Campus Lutheran Chapel and Student Center, built in 1965 at Birchwood St. and Ellis Av., where you enter the upper campus near the hilltop.

*   *   *   *

Descending the hill, you might easily be attracted by a rare old house labeled Blue Earth County Museum at 606 Broad St., two blocks east of Front St., the main business street.

Rensselaer D. Hubbard, president of the Hubbard Milling Co., built it in 1871, furnished it lavishly, and lived there. It has mellow old silk tapestry wallcovering and some of the original furnishing, such as India brass lamps that Hubbard bought in New Orleans with a lot of other things during the Reconstruction period.

You will find further: an excellent Indian collection, a carved stairwell, an Edison gramophone, a rosewood piano, a 1900 music box, Tiffany lights, marble fireplaces and too much else to list.

*   *   *   *

I urge you to look at the falls at Minneopa State Park, about 3 miles south of Mankato just west of Hwy. 169.

I also took a run 5 miles south on Hwy. 169 to the Rapidan turn-off and then east a couple of miles to Rapidan to see the falls there. The falls were nice, but they were hard to see because the power company had everything fenced off.

VALLEYS
Trip No. 7 / Zumbro Falls and Millville

WANT TO RELAX? Go to the fertile valley. The crack of the bat will be heard Sunday afternoon in Zumbro Falls.

There are major leagues, minor leagues and the Wabasha County League (Millville, Zumbrota, West Florence, Mazeppa, Bellechester and Zumbro Falls.)

There aren't any bleachers. You can sit in your car, or you can stand on the sidelines down there on the flats between the Zumbro River bluffs.

The ball game by no means is the only reason you should try to go. Skip the game and you're still a winner. On the drive into Zumbro Falls from Wabasha via Hwy. 60, there are long views and there is burgeoning green — up hill and down dale past good farms, healthy farm animals and here and there a mossy log rotting in the valley.

Those stumps where some trees have been logged and others left standing — that's walnut. The Sportsmen's Club wants to plant more in the Valley.

*   *   *   *

Downstream from Zumbro Falls at Millville Stephen E. Appel pointed with pride.

High on the sandstone bluff overlooking the village on the Zumbro River he pointed out a white wooden gauge, about 15 feet tall, on which a marker was suspended by a rope.

"The rope goes over a pulley," Appel explained. "At the other end is a keg floating in the water back in the rock. There's a big 20-by-20-foot cavity chiseled out of the rock and that's our water reservoir. We watch the gauge and when the water gets low, we just pump some more up the hill into the reservoir. Have we got water pressure!"

Before I left his place Appel handed me a paper bag with two rutabagas in it.

Millville's unusual water reservoir dates back to around the turn of the century. I learned this when I called on Mayor Karl W. Schumacher.

His wife, the granddaughter of Charles H. Read, Mill-

ville's first postmaster (Millville was founded around 1870) had recollections that were fresh and interesting.

"There was a little short Irishman named William McGuigan, who came back from Montana," Mrs. Schumacher said. "He worked out there with the miners. His father, J. F., owned the general store here in Millville.

"William said the rock up there might make a good place to store the water, and everybody laughed at him. What did a little Irishman know? But he was used to mining methods. He climbed up and tested the rock, and then he started drilling. And he did the whole thing himself. That was around 1900."

Removal of the village's only railroad, which came up the Zumbro Valley, first on narrow and later on standard gauge tracks, hurt the town, she said.

"Before the railroad left we had two hotels, two grain elevators, two grocery and drug stores and a bank."

It might have hurt the town, but the old railroad grade now rebuilt into a gravel road makes one of the prettiest drives along a valley bottom that anyone could ask. I followed it eastward from Zumbro Falls to Millville and beyond.

It took me into Hwy. 60, on which I turned right for a scenic ride into Wabasha.

But take a look around Millville before you leave it —peer through the windows of its tiny "city hall," and you'll see some old firehose carts, still used on occasion, although fire departments come in from nearby towns. There is a small park with picnic tables behind some sheds overlooking the river road. If you feel like climbing, it is possible to tramp up an old overgrown wagon trail to the top of the bluff. Even if you only feel like driving around town, signs of the venerable past do not escape the eye.

VALLEYS
Trip No. 8 / Plum City

THERE IS A gem of a small town just off Hwy. 10 where it runs southeast through western Wisconsin.

It is Plum City 70 miles southeast of Minneapolis.

It has the finest small park of any town its size (population 384) that I have seen. The park's central attraction is a clear springfed pond whose water is channeled into nearby Plum Creek, a tributary of the Chippewa River. The park has a historical past.

*   *   *   *

Excerpt from sign in the park: ". . . As to this beautiful spring, there is an argument as to whether it is natural or partially excavated. At least it was here when the English took possession in 1761."

The town began during the French occupation. The French took fur out through the St. Croix waterways to Lake Superior. Before that the Sioux and Chippewas fought over the valley hunting grounds.

*   *   *   *

Townsmen stock the springfed pond with big rainbow trout. Fishing is verboten, but once in a while a trout is seen with a leader hanging from its mouth.

Mallards also are brought in. Right now there are four hens and a drake. Three of the hens are nesting and one has some "little peepers," in the words of Jack Van, proprietor of Van's cafe across the street.

The hens nest in weeds and bushes around the pond, and one is in an oil drum, set on planks in the water for this purpose.

Van, born in Plum City, was a Chicago contract en-

gineer. One day when he found himself getting annoyed because another fellow had taken his usual seat on the commuter train he said, "I decided that I was *really* in a rut."

But he knew where there was a nicer one. Every idyllic small town in a valley has got to have one tall tapered church steeple standing against the greenery, and Plum City has one.

It also has three other churches, a city-owned 35-bed hospital ("Just approved for Medicare," boasts Van), a priceless museum piece of a red fire house with a belfry and embossed tin siding, a larger Legion park on Plum Creek, and a beaver dam.

"Some of the people here want to tear down the old fire house," Van said. "I'm trying to talk them out of it."

They might take a lesson from the people of Zermatt, Switzerland, who were smart enough to preserve their old log granaries as tourist attractions.

*   *   *   *

For high views of Plum City there are steep roads up the surrounding hills. One of these, blacktopped, you will find by taking the first turn to the right off the main street as you go south past the Catholic church, the one with the tall steeple. It's called Blue Goose hill.

Tourists like to photograph a Plum City sign which reads: "Office Entrance . . . John C. Doctor, M.D. . . . C. W. Doctor, M.D." John C. is C. W's father.

VALLEYS

Trip No. 9 / Moosehorn, Kettle, and Snake

SERENDIPITY MAY WORK for you as it did for me on a jaunt up Hwy. 61 to Moose Lake, Minn.

My destination was a canoe-access point which, the Moosehorn Rod and Gun Club had informed me, was opening on the Moosehorn River on the south edge of Moose Lake.

I had little trouble finding the access, a quarter of a mile west of Hwy. 61 just before you cross the bridge over the Moosehorn.

     *   *   *   *

They aren't trying to start a hot white-water course for rapids-shooters but rather a family-fun course. Increased talk about canoeing, and noticing how many cars are carrying canoes, gave the club the idea.

They're working on the first leg, downstream to Willow River, Minn., where the Moosehorn enters the Kettle River. They plan to clear portage paths in three places and put up some picnic tables along the way.

They expect eventually to extend their good offices downstream along the Kettle.

     *   *   *   *

After sizing up the Moosehorn access, I stopped at several other places along the Hwy. 61 trail (some of it now Interstate Hwy. 35) and found plenty of leisure activity, especially at Sandstone and Pine City, Minn.

     *   *   *   *

At Sandstone a short jog east on Hwy. 123 will take you to Robinson Park on the Kettle River. A sign points to the left just before you cross the Kettle.

This is a fascinating park, for it is located on the site

of an old quarry from which sandstone was taken for many buildings still standing around the state. You still can see foundations and a concrete apron for the mill which provided the quarry with stone-cutting power.

There were quite a number of campers and fishermen in this city-maintained park.

Lawrence J. Dahl of Chisago City, Minn., was holding up a big, heavy snapping turtle by the tail and trying to decide how to keep it alive until he got it back to a friend who had promised to cook the first snapper Dahl brought him.

It had appeared on the shoreline where Mrs. Dahl had a small northern pike on a stringer.

Before the snapper could eat the northern, Dahl got a .22-caliber pistol out of his camper and put a bullet through the turtle's neck. That slowed it down a little, but it was still alive straining to get a snap at somebody.

Dahl finally solved the transportation problem by swinging it by the tail through a low cabinet door in his camper and quickly clamping shut the door.

* * * *

Farther south at Pine City, where Hwy. 61 crosses the Snake River, I found activity at a long familiar spot, the dock behind Harold Carl's Riverside Sport Shop.

Some were struggling to get an outboard motor going. Others were trying their luck around the floating dock and from shore.

VALLEYS
Trip No. 10 / Pierz

PIERZ, MINN., HAS an interesting recreational history. Here a timely investment coupled with foresight brightened the whole face of a community.

Pierz has a population of about 800. It was about the same size in the depression '30s. But then its recreational facilities consisted of one not too accessible small lake 3 miles out of town.

Today it has one of the prettiest swimming holes I ever saw just half a mile from the main street. It has picnic tables and acres of green beneath big trees. It has a playground and a busy nine-hole golf course with freshly watered grass greens and fairways running beside and across a creek and between beautiful stands of tall Norway pines.

At 1 p.m. on any hot sunny day the swimmers begin to gather at the swimming hole — mostly kids, but some adults, too. It is a municipal swimming hole, belonging to Pierz, and it is just below the joining of the Skunk River and the Little Hillman (both just country creeks at this point).

It is there, and so is the green grass which covers the park and the golf course, because Pierz residents back in the 30's had enough foresight to invest in a dam. The federal Work Projects Administration (WPA) furnished the labor. Pierz bought the land (80 acres of pasture) and supplied the materials.

Mornings Fred Boiko, Pierz bowling alley operator, coaches the Little League (he once played pro ball in the St. Louis Browns' chain) and afternoons he is the swimming instructor at the Pierz swimming hole.

Back before the Pierz people made a big decision there probably would have been little to attract Boiko to the town. Today its golf course register carries names and addresses from Wisconsin, Iowa, Missouri and all over the Midwest. Tourists drive 30 miles west from Mille Lacs and from other directions to play its picturesque course. It brings people into town.

It didn't just happen. It took planning, hoping and persuasion. It started when Fred Preinesberger was a boy hunting crows in the pasture where the course now stands. He dreamed about making a park out of it, but later he became a golf enthusiast and manager of a lumber yard. There were only two other golfers in town— the dentist, Dr. F. L. Zehnpfennig, and the banker, A. P. Stoll, president of the Farmers and Merchants Bank.

For years this trio played courses at places like Long

Prairie, Little Falls, Brainerd, Sauk Centre and Willmar, sized them up and dreamed of the day when Pierz might have its own.

Came the depression and WPA. The three put their pet project in front of the voters. The citizens of Pierz approved. Things got under way. The streams were dammed, pipes and pumps installed for the water. Before too long Stoll, Zehnpfennig and Preinesberger were teeing off on the course of their dreams.

Although the pipes were laid early, it wasn't until 1950 when Preinesberger took over as course superintendent and dug up the old pipe connections, that fairway watering began.

Until then it hadn't been considered practical, but Preinesberger, noting how business was increasing, put everything under sprinklers. Today the whole place looks like a park in the Emerald City of Oz, and patronage is growing faster than ever.

To find Pierz, take Hwy. 10 through Elk River to Becker and turn right on Hwy. 25. It will take you to Pierz.

Along the way you'll find what I consider a truly great name of a town — Jakeville. Being a country jake at heart, I plan to retire there.

Right now it consists of a store and a dance hall. The place is named after the store's original owner, Jake Ziwicke, a bachelor.

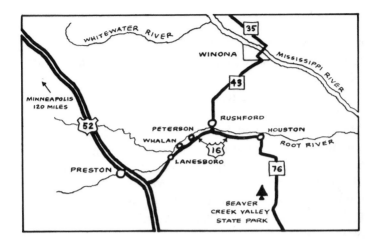

VALLEYS

Trip No. 11 / Root River Country

To SPEAK IN superlatives (and why not) the acme of pastoral charm is to be found along the Root river in southeastern Minnesota.

After a rainy June I don't think I saw a dry blade of grass in the whole area—miles of solid green.

It was raining lightly part of the time. In that country a certain intermittent mistiness can be counted as a romantic asset as it hangs over the distant hills, bluishly, and occasionally fogs up the valleys.

A high school exchange teacher from East Cotting-with, Yorkshire, remarked that if one could drive direct-ly from part of Minnesota into parts of England, one wouldn't know the difference. This could be one of those parts.

Starting at Preston, 120 road miles south of Minne-apolis on United States highway 52, one may go up-stream or down. For a short prelude I took a country road following South Branch Root a few miles upstream (southwest). The road climbs a hill and affords a wide view.

There's something to be said for seeing miles of hilly countryside, groves, fields, meadows and grazing cattle from a country road but the highway, too, has its advantages. These are to be found by branching off United States highway 52 northeastward on U. S. highway 16 about three miles southeast of Preston. This road follows the Root through Lanesboro, Whalan, Peterson, Rushford and Houston ("not Texas," as a sign outside of town says).

Before reaching Lanesboro you follow a high ridge from which one can view what appears to be the promised land stretching out on all sides. On the left the highway department provides a roadside parking area and picnic grounds before the descent. Stop by all means.

On the way down into the Root valley you'll see on the right a sign, "State Fishery," with an arrow. This is another worthwhile stop. It's Minnesota's biggest trout hatchery. The second largest is one on the Whitewater river.

The one at hand is only a quarter of a mile off the highway. You'll see rows of shed-covered tanks where the fingerlings live. Step up to an open door and you'll be surprised at the density of fish per cubic foot. Then you'll see that it isn't that thick throughout the tank.

The fish gather at your first appearance. They bump and roll over one another, like chickens or ducks crowding around to be fed. The big ones in the pond do the same thing when you walk to the water's edge.

A trout research biologist told me it takes the trout about two days to get over this tameness when they're turned loose.

This hatchery has a capacity of 45 to 50 thousand pounds of fish a year. Usually that means about a million fingerlings and 160 thousand trout of catchable size (20 months old). At the hatchery they get vegetable protein mixed with a little liver and fish meal. The hatchery raises brown, brook (speckled) and rainbow trout. The brown trout go mostly into southeastern Minnesota streams.

For further enjoyment simply follow the Root. I'd advise you to turn off the highway and drive over narrow bridges into the towns of Whalan and Peterson. If you are a connoisseur of small towns, you know that a small town loses something when a highway goes through it.

At Houston I turned right off highway 16 on to Minnesota highway 76, which goes to Beaver Creek Valley state park. By walking three-quarters of a mile from the parking lot (after hopping from rock to rock over Beaver creek) you'll find the head of the creek where it comes right out of the rocks. Watercress grows in the stream. (Don't pick it.)

This is rattle snake country, but the park superintendent's wife told me she's never seen one in the valley. She wouldn't advise much hill climbing, unless you're prepared, though. That's where the snake hunters go, and she understands they had pretty good luck near the park this spring. They went into the rocks on the hills with their pronged sticks and came out with a dozen or more rattlers.

If you want a different way home try state highway 43 to Winona and cross the Mississippi to return on Wisconsin 35 to Red Wing.

VALLEYS

Trip No. 12 / Ortonville

IN SEPTEMBER I took a drive around the hills of Ortonville, on the east shore of Big Stone lake, which is a wide place in the Minnesota River on the western boundary of Minnesota. It is well worth your time.

A meander around the city and 10 miles northwestward along the Minnesota side of Big Stone lake is mighty pretty driving.

The lake has a frank open-faced character which differs from the withdrawn, somewhat haughty pulchritude of some of our northern lakes. Some of its shoreline is quite open and grassy. The trees are big elms, willows, cottonwood and oaks.

Some of the land along the shore northwest of the city is given over to apple orchards, and the apples are for

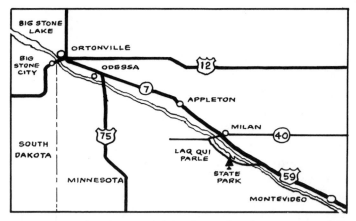

sale. There is plenty of lakeshore development — big houses and shady lawns with sedate lawn furniture in the city, cottages and resorts farther out.

Any town, of course, that has high hills overlooking water, like some of the St. Croix valley towns, for example, has an atmospheric head start, and Ortonville has a good one.

It abounds in magnificent views of Big Stone lake, if you look for them. Since they are west-facing views, I'm sure that few cities are so well-situated for the admiration of sunsets. (There might be a slogan in this sunset view angle.)

The thing to do while driving around town is to watch for turns up the hill. One of them, just north of town, takes you to the golf course, arranged on a kind of plateau where, I understand, many a ball is irretrievably lost by going out of bounds over the bank.

Nelson Park is another pretty lookout on the hilltop, right in town. Along the lakeshore near the business section the city has very thoughtfully provided a grassy park and bathing beach. Many a municipality has lived to regret a lack of this kind of foresight.

39

High and east of town where highways 12 and 75 meet is a 115-ton granite monolith standing on four granite pillars and labeled Paul Bunyan's anchor. You might hesitate to sit at one of the picnic tables beneath this scary weight, but you'll want to size it up as a proud specimen of the Ortonville granite whose quarries and broad outcroppings south of town interest geologists.

Before heading southeast it won't hurt to drive across the bridge to Big Stone City, S. D. There are some nice views there, too, and surely it wouldn't do to get this close to South Dakota without crossing the line.

Heading southeastward, take highway 75 to Odessa, highway 7 to Appleton and Milan. At Milan turn right on highway 40, which takes one on a causeway across some marshland and then on a bridge across Lac Qui Parle. Soon after crossing the bridge turn left on a gravel road which goes along the southwest shore of Lac Qui Parle.

Keep to the left and you'll go through the state park and across the dam at the southeast end of the lake. Before crossing the dam, notice on the left a parking area with tables and a shelter.

Beneath the latter is an interesting, if somewhat worn and sandy, scale model of the Laq Qui Parle flood control and conservation project.

There is an enlightening explanatory plaque here, written by Adolph F. Meyer, Minneapolis hydrological authority. It tells how to regulate the water level if anything should happen to those in control.

After you cross the dam, to the left is the Lac Qui Parle mission site, marked by signs. Get out and have a look. You'll see a restored mission. Rustic plaques will tell you that Alexander Huggins, Sarah Poage, Stephen R. Riggs, Samuel and Gideon Pond, Jonas Pettijohn and

40

others labored at the mission until it was abandoned in 1835.

They will point out homesites, cabinsites, burial grounds and a steep path of stepping stones into a shadowy ravine where the mission spring once flowed.

The grounds here are equipped with picnic tables and a hikers' resting bench up on the hill behind the mission.

From Milan you may head due east along highway 40 toward Minneapolis or go southeast along highway 59 to Montevideo, which has some of the nicest riverside parks you could ask for, running right through the middle of town.

VALLEYS
Trip No. 13 / Theilman

READER'S TIP (on file for some time): "Your account of Stockholm, Wis., reminded me of a delightful out-of-the-way town . . . Theilman, Minn. . . . 10 or 15 miles southwest of Wabasha . . . most interesting general store . . . as a souvenir I bought a cow tail holder."

On the trail of the above lead I had a relaxing ride west on Hwy. 60 from Wabasha up the valley of the Zumbro River. The leaves are a bit somber this year, but the ride was none the less enjoyable.

At about 10 miles out of Wabasha I turned left or south on Wabasha County Road 13. A leafy descent 3.5 miles into the valley brought me to County Road 4, on which I turned left a short way into Theilman, just short of the bridge.

To the left of the road and somewhat above it so that one could not see it too well, I found a sleepy town, a very few blocks in size, surrounded by fall woods and hills.

I recognized the general store as the first two-story frame building on the main street, adjacent to a smaller brick building on the corner labeled Theilman Bank.

The bank had become a warehouse. Through the windows one saw stacked grain sacks. It was past noon, but the store was locked, so I repaired to a cottage-like tavern at the far end of the street. Here I learned that the store would reopen at 1 p.m. Meanwhile at the bar I nosed through a well-worn History of Wabasha County. Therein I read that:

Christian Theilman platted the town in 1877 and got the Chicago, Milwaukee & St. Paul Railway to stop there (the line up the Zumbro has since been removed).

In January 1878 Peter Hall built the store mentioned by my tipster, "a commodious two-story frame," the town's first building. Later that year William Morris built a blacksmith shop and Henry Sommerhelder a wagon shop. In the fall up popped the first luxuries, two saloons.

The Theilman Bank was incorporated June 1, 1911, with a capital stock of $10,000 and Theodore Hampe as president (Henry Theilman vice president). In 1920, when the history was published, deposits were $321,000 and the statement showed a surplus of $11,500.

After returning to the store and finding it locked, I followed Mrs. Radamacher's directions and tried a tidy white house with window boxes on the other side of the block. A genial lady who turned out to be Mrs. Albert Hampe, the store owner's wife, admitted me and awakened her equally genial husband, who had been taking a nap on the davenport.

He laughed heartily at my tipster's letter. "I know this fellow," he said. "He's an old friend of mine. I remember his visit here. He thumped all the commode pots in the store trying to get one that went 'Bong!' "

A cow tail holder, he explained, is used to keep the tail from slapping milkers in the face. The store, however, is no antique shop, and for lack of demand the tail holders have not been restocked. Hampe pointed to a large two-man saw. "Another dead item," he said. "Everything's power now."

He carried, however, an active stock of horse hardware (eveners, tug-chains), some hay pulleys, heavy hooks for log chains, cow hooks (to keep them from jumping fences), overalls, work shoes, work rubbers, samples of hybrid seed corn and, of course, a full line of groceries.

Albert Hampe's father was the first and only president of the Theilman Bank.

The bank, after the Depression bank "holiday," returned its depositors 85 cents on the dollar—considerably better than many. "It was a shame," Hampe said. "The bank was required to sell its bonds, which were paying 5 and 6 per cent interest, at the worst possible time. If it could have held them for another six months, it could have returned 100 per cent instead of 85."

The closing of the bank, he opined, was a worse blow to Theilman than the removal of the railroad, but he blames neither for the town's decline, which he feels was bound to come.

The town flourished, he said, at a time when two miles of grain-hauling took half an hour. Theilman's three grain elevators were handy, and their prices were better than many.

Today, trucks haul the grain, and passenger cars whisk people to a wide variety of shopping centers.

VALLEYS

Trip No. 14 / Welch

AT FIRST, WELCH, a very small town in the valley of the Cannon River, seems a charming, sleepy place. It is charming, all right, but its residents soon disclose that there is plenty going on to occupy the energy and the imagination.

For instance, they are nearing the climax of the horseshoe pitching season and have two recreational enterprises—three, if you count the tree house which I found some boys building across the road from Mrs. Earl Montey's Cannon River Inn.

One of the boys (Darnell Montey) was her son. Mrs. Montey is a widow who collects Indian arrowheads, some of them from the Cannon valley, and is something of an amateur photographer. A hand-colored enlargement of one of her bird's-eye views of Welch and the river, taken from a high hill, hangs on the inn wall. Admirers of it have bought several copies.

Another boy in the tree house (David Kruse) was the son of Edward M. Kruse, captain of the Welch horseshoe pitching team.

Kruse, who grew up in nearby Miesville, has thrown as many as 33 ringers in a game (50 shoes are thrown in a regulation game).

Welch is holding its own in some mighty fast company. The final match of the season (unless it results in a league tie) will be against Randolph on the Welch courts, right by the Welch bridge over the Cannon River, where the Welch pitchers keep their hands in, summer and winter.

Horseshoes are a tradition-hallowed recreation around Welch, however, and I mentioned some new enterprises. One of these is "Hidden Valley."

It is about 150 acres of rolling woods and meadows along the south bank of the Cannon River, part of a 300-acre farm owned by Gilbert A. Axelson, known as "Gib." It is in operation as a camp ground.

Gib has piped in water, put through roads to the various campsites, done some decorative planning, set out some shiny new refuse cans and with the help of relatives built, stained and installed 40 stout picnic tables.

Gib's sister, Mrs. Richard Scrivner, and husband have started the Welch Stables next to the camp grounds.

There are seven Scrivners in all, Tim, Abigail, Donald,

Joe, Sandra, Billy, and parents. The stable's current specialty is "guided scenic trail rides on gentle saddle horses" with Abigail in the lead. In winter there are sleigh rides.

Downstream I found a couple fishing by the dam.

Most of the people who fish there aren't aware that they're on Clarence Nelson's land. He owns both sides of the river near his feed mill and other lands up and down the valley where his family has lived since the 1880s.

He closed his feed mill in 1965 and threatened to push it into the Cannon River if the assessor didn't lower its tax evaluation, but he is generally benevolent.

He never bothers fishermen. He advises young men to pay off their debts, avoid bankruptcy, protect their credit and believe in the living Christ. He takes an active interest in the valley's growth and his sons, Clem and Leigh, run the Welch Village Ski Area.

(On October 8, 1968, after the above was written, Clarence Nelson died at the Mayo Clinic. He was 75. Clem, Leigh and their mother still live in the valley.)

CHAPTER III   MISSISSIPPI RIVER

Trip No. 15 / Hastings Lock Number Two

SOMETIMES THE MISSISSIPPI opens earlier than usual. When it does, March twentieth or thereabouts can be an exciting time to watch the barges come up the river.

Sometimes with snow still on the ground barge connoisseurs will drive a bit upriver from Hastings, Minn., to watch the action at U. S. Lock and Dam No. 2.

The observation platform at No. 2 is one of the best for viewing. It is closer to the lock pond than the one at Alma, Wis., for example, which stands back about 40 feet. At Hastings you are almost hanging over the barges when they go through.

This is not the earliest, but one of the earlier seasons for river traffic. The earliest in the memory of John R. Brewer, lockmaster at No. 2 just upstream from Hastings, was in 1964.

That year Mississippi traffic started March 7 at Hastings, and consequently March 1964 saw nearly a normal summer month's commercial volume. Pleasure craft traffic never amounts to much until June. It adds up to a little better than 5,000 boats in an average summer.

Brewer, 56, has been working on the river since he was 17. He was born in Diamond Bluff, Wis., on the Mississippi.

His father was dredgemaster on the Army Engineer Corps dredge *Pelee,* and John's first job was behind a barrow, wheeling coal from a barge across on planks to the dredge's steam engine.

His brother Roy, now retired, succeeded his father as dredgemaster and John has been a lockmaster at different locks for about 30 years.

The spring of 1965 was one of the worst for traffic on the Mississippi; in fact, there wasn't any through the months of March and April.

After a late breakup came the floods, and water reached a record high at No. 2—10.55 feet above the normal level of the upper pool. The locks were useless because the water was over the handrails along the walls which contain the whole system.

Lockmaster and crew were busy piling sandbags around the powerhouse and office and 14 pumps were burning up three barrels of gasoline a day to carry off the seepage. John used a rowboat to get from the locks to his house, which also was surrounded.

It finally leveled off on Easter Sunday.

"What a relief that was," recalled John.

*　　　*　　　*　　　*

To find Lock and Dam No. 2 follow the black-lettered signs on white background, the first of which points upstream at the Hastings end of the Hwy. 61 bridge over the Mississippi. It's 1.3 miles from this turnoff.

You can get a high view of it from Law's Nursery west of Hwy. 61 on the high bank across the river.

*　　　*　　　*　　　*

A barge and the boat that pushes it through the lock are, together, twice as long as a football field.

Barges carry about 10 million tons of cargo through the locks in a season.

The average load on a coal barge is 1,200 tons.

MISSISSIPPI RIVER
Trip No. 16 / Upper Locks, Minneapolis

THE BIG ONE: The Mississippi River's Upper Lock (and dam) in Minneapolis is worth looking at.

It not only lifts boats higher than any other lock on the Mississippi, it lifts them higher than any single lock in the Panama Canal.

Its lift is 49.2 feet. The locks on the Atlantic end of the Panama Canal lift 28.3 feet each, and at the Pacific end they vary from 25 to around 40.

The Upper Lock is also a lot faster. It fills or empties in eight minutes. In Panama the up or down speed is two feet a minute.

Figures on the combined lift of Mississippi River locks are also impressive. The Panama Canal's summit level is 85 feet above sea level. In Minneapolis the combined lift of Upper, Lower and Ford Dam locks is 112 feet.

The 22 locks between Minneapolis and St. Louis lift boats 420 feet, only 27 feet shy of the Foshay Tower's height.

If you've looked down into many locks, you'll appreciate the depth of the Upper Lock in Minneapolis. From its observation platform you can also enjoy a panoramic view of St. Anthony Falls, the river, its banks and various bridges.

People are appreciating this view every day, but an odd and bothersome thing to Harry Shulz, assistant lockmaster, is that most of the viewers are tourists. Where are the Minneapolitans?

"We *want* people to come and look. We *welcome* them," said Shulz. School teachers from Wisconsin and

other fringe points trot kids through the place in droves, but the locals, even those who live only a few blocks away, don't seem to know it's there.

It goes without saying that neither do they know it was selected by an outside panel as the Chief of Army Corps of Engineers Distinguished Achievement for 1966.

The Upper Lock and Dam is prepared to receive visitors. Ceramic tile rest rooms. Drinking fountains. A guest register. A roomy platform with broad views up-river, downriver and across. A historical plaque that runs about 1,500 words and covers 11 points of interest.

Longest plaque I ever saw.

*   *   *   *

You can find the Upper Lock by turning southeast or downriver as close to downtown end of the Third Av. Bridge as you can get. Or, if there aren't any trains in the way and you don't mind bumping over a lot of tracks you can follow Portland Av. all the way to the river.

Once in the parking lot, you'll find the observation tower door by walking southeast or downriver and looking behind the first corner you come to.

*   *   *   *

The upper harbor is not yet developed very much, but here is an average summer month's traffic through the Upper Lock: 64 towboats, 104 barges, 73 pleasure boats.

*   *   *   *

The Lower Lock, near the Cedar Av. Bridge, is almost as new as the Upper Lock but doesn't afford nearly as good a view. Hence, it has no observation platform. The pillars of the 35-W bridge run just a bit downstream of the Lower Lock.

MISSISSIPPI RIVER
Trip No. 17 / The Source

I RAN INTO this kid at the headwaters of the Mississippi in Itasca State Park.

He was aiming a little box camera at other kids running across the Mississippi on rocks.

"Do you mind if I take a picture of you taking a picture?" I asked.

"Swell," he said and jumped into action. "Fall in!" he kept yelling at the kids on the rocks as he aimed his camera, but nobody would.

In fact they kept waving their arms to keep their balance and, strangely enough, they kept it.

The man who seemed to be in charge of all the action and stood watchfully by turned out to be Harold O. Folkestad, principal of the Randall, Minn., Junior High School.

The youthful photographer was one of 50 seventh graders on their annual class picnic.

"They raise the money for it themselves," Folkestad said.

"How?" I asked, as a swarm of kids tried to scramble across the headwaters on rocks and others scurried back on a plank bridge a little way downstream.

"I don't know," he said. "I guess with popcorn. Jim, how did you raise the money this year?"

"Selling popcorn and candy bars at the games," Jim said.

"Well, we've got to move on," the principal said. "We try to hit all the high spots. Let's go!" he called.

I stepped aside just in time to avoid the stampede back to the bus.

Itasca State Park is a resort par excellence for the sight-seer:

One may rent canoes or boats on Lake Itasca.

There are many picnic tables.

There is a 15-mile scenic drive around the park, part of it through a deep forest.

Douglas Lodge at the south end of the lake holds about a hundred overnight guests and serves meals on the European plan (rooms and meals separate). The lodge is open. For reservations one may write Douglas Lodge, Lake Itasca, Minn., or call 218-266-3601.

MISSISSIPPI RIVER

Trip No. 18 / McGregor

NORTHEASTERN IOWA IS ESPECIALLY interesting for its Mississippi river towns, like McGregor, and the Mississippi tributaries—the Shell Rock (on which Mason City has a versatile recreational park), the Cedar running by Nashua, the Wapsipinicon, the zig-zag Turkey, and the Upper Iowa.

My wife and I drove through this country eastward from Mason City to McGregor. Making a difficult choice, we picked a southerly route through Nashua instead of northerly through Decorah with the Norwegian Museum, which we hope to see another time.

We went east and southeast on U.S. Hwy. 18 and then 218 into Nashua, thence northeast on Hwy. 346 across the Cedar River. The highway took us within 75 feet of the front door of the Little Brown Church in the Vale, the inspiration for an old song of the same name. The church is pleasantly situated among tall pine trees and seems to be functioning well. Many baptisms and marriages are performed in this Congregational church, open to all.

Continuing east, Hwy. 346 took us into Hwy. 18 again and east into West Union, then northeast to Clermont on the Turkey River. We had an excellent lunch in the town's hotel, across the street from the Historical Museum. We stayed in a motel at the foot of McGregor's fascinating old rivertown main street. On the water side of the

railroad tracks near the rip-rapped riverbank, our lodgings were about 15 feet above water level.

McGregor tourists take side trips to such places as Guttenberg downstream, Effigy Mounds National Monument upstream, Decorah inland and other points marked on tourist maps within that radius. For my part I contentedly walked up one side of McGregor's main street and down the other.

Once called "Pocket City" because of its pocketlike place among the big river bluffs, the town was named McGregor after a river-shipping grain merchant. Its inhabitants respect its architecture.

At the river end of the main street stands a small but dignified old hotel, now a private residence, painted grey with black trim. A neatly painted wooden plaque reads: "1856—Frontier Landmark Hotel from Pre-Civil War. Fancy dining—staircase and halls echo footsteps of great and small . . . the great river carried all . . . restored 1967."

The Frontier is occupied by John Bickel, successful real estate dealer and father of Herb and Dan Bickel, who carry on the trade while their father sparkplugs an ongoing movement to preserve and shine up McGregor's valuable antiquity.

"Office and home of Diamond Joe Reynolds, early grain buyer. . ." says a legend by a "Pizza P.O." parlor with its old post office furnishings shined up.

Other evidence of tourist orientation includes signs like "The Stone Balloon" (an arts and crafts shop), "The Old Time Shoppe," "The Emporium—Antiques," "Accent Galore—Plaster Arts, Gifts," and "Sea Shell Shop—Souvenirs."

If antiquity eventually gets to you, you can take a quick drive just two miles south on Hwy. 340, which leads high on the bluff to Pike's Peak State Park.

However, perhaps nothing will stir your river-loving blood like a riverboat pushing a barge upchannel right past your motel at night digging up a wake, lights aglow, and searchlight stabbing alternate shores. The whole big complex moves surely, penetratingly, upstream.

MISSISSIPPI RIVER

Trip No. 19 / Lake Pepin

THE LAKE CITY MARINA, which claims "the world's largest fishing barge" and could for all I know be the world's largest municipally operated inland marina, has always fascinated me.

It's a jazzy place always full of glamorous crafts with its own built-up, tree-studded mobile home peninsula on one side of the inlet and a sailors' clubhouse and marina manager's office on the other.

I thought I had been noticing an increase in the proportion of sailboats docked in the marina, and harbormaster Ben Simons confirmed it.

In 1970 there were only 25 sailboats in the marina. Now there are 120. The marina has 388 "slips," each holding a boat, and there is quite a waiting list. On it, the sailboats outnumber the motorboats three to one. Ten years ago, the ratio was reversed.

There are still a lot of fancy cruisers in the marina, and there undoubtedly will continue to be. Jim Marland, marina gas pumper, said his customers are hunting for gas bargains but aren't doing a lot of complaining. But, he said, "People are beginning to find out how good sailing is on lake Pepin." It's over 20 miles long and 1½ to 3 miles wide.

Marland said the sailors are saving money, all right.

An average 26-foot Lake Pepin sloop might cost somewhere between $18,000 and $22,000 equipped, but with
a cruiser you figure about $1,000 a foot.

Simons said that the marina could take in another 100
sailboats next season if it had the room. There's a chance
the room might be doubled,

The Army Corps of Engineers is making a big survey
on the feasibility of doubling the harbor by taking the
bottleneck out of the entryway and relocating it downstream. It would mean putting in a second breakwater
from the mobile home point southeastward to form a
harbor opening in conjunction with a breakwater now
extending from the mainland.

Once I took a Lake Pepin excursion cruise on John Halager's *Chicago Queen*. Now I can report on a Lake Pepin sailing cruise.

Skiing pal Walter J. Peterson, St. Croix Falls, and I joined four other guests and Ralph Smith on Ralph's 26-foot fixed-keel sloop, complete with cabin, toilet, and auxiliary motor.

The motor got us out of the harbor, Ralph took the tiller, the sails filled, and we got that surge of wind-power and boat-tilting that packs its own kick. Soon we were involved in the rope pulling, winch winding, and side changing that makes one feel important—part of the action.

We had one mishap. During a come-about and tilt change the telephoto lens came loose from a guest's camera and fell in the river. We drifted back over the general area, and with his electronic sounder Ralph checked the depth at 17 feet.

Recovery of anything black on the murky bottom was impossible. General commiseration turned to a lifting of spirits as we tacked north against a brisk wind under a clear sky.

We passed Point No Point at Frontenac and eventually turned south with the wind.

It was fun viewing the scenic rock outcropping along the Wisconsin side from this vantage point where the bluffs look higher than from land, and it was fun looking at the other boats, some with big colored spinnakers, some riding with the wind "wing and wing" (sails out on both sides).

Above a point just two miles above Lake City we anchored right by some beached cruisers and went swimming—cool, nice.

CHAPTER IV   MILLS

Trip No. 20 / Phelps Mill on the Ottertail

PHELPS MILL IS on the Otter Tail River about 12 miles northeast of Fergus Falls and about eight northwest of Battle Lake, where Geneva Tweten (pronounced "Tweetin") was born.

The mill is the nucleus of a new county park, a development which can in great measure be attributed to Miss Tweten's efforts. She lives and works as a dressmaker above the radio station, a two-story brick building at 112½ Lincoln Av. near the center of Fergus Falls.

Civic pride, ambition and accomplishment abound in this Otter Tail County seat, and Miss Tweten embodies them all. When she was a little girl, she played at Phelps Mill.

During a 1921 Fourth of July celebration she was "Courage" in an historic pageant of Otter Tail County and Fergus Falls. When she was somewhat older, she was one of two bathing beauties whose photographs appeared on the cover of a tourist folder for the area.

Phelps Mill began grinding wheat into flour for the farmers in 1889 and it was still running in 1921, although no longer so fast and furiously.

Trains were taking wheat to bigger mills. In 1894 the mill ground 44,000 bushels of wheat and 25,000 of feed. It had a barn to accommodate farmers from far away and a house for staying overnight when the line of teams waiting at the mill was too long.

By 1921 business was well on the downgrade. In 1919 William E. Thomas, the original owner, sold the mill to a co-op and moved to California. In 1927 the co-op sold it to Halvor Evenson. Evenson ran it until 1931. Thereafter it stood idle.

When a building like that stands idle, deterioration sets in and vandalism follow. Geneva Tweten couldn't stand to see it happen. She approached Evenson on an asking price ($20,000). She went to the federal government, she went to the state, and she went to the county.

Everybody agreed that the old mill should be preserved, but nobody did anything. After about seven years of this, she was making a routine check with Evenson to see how he stood on price and got the surprise of her life. It had shrunk to $3,500.

This time the county sprang into action, bought the mill, acquired some more land for a 40-acre park along the shady, verdant banks of the Ottertail, and, with the help of the federal Green Thumb project for workers over 65, has opened the mill to the public and built a picnic ground with well, pump, tables, fireplaces and outhouses.

This is the first step in an ambitious park project which in a few years may have the mill back in working order, plus a swimming pool, a three-hole golf course, camp grounds and room for softball, horseshoes, badminton and volleyball.

Now Miss Tweten cuts a dress pattern on the table in her working-living room above the radio station, surrounded by her books, her paintings (two of Phelps Mill) and momentos of the past.

She is afraid some of the Phelps Mill park plans are a little too fancy and modern and wishes that a more old-time atmosphere could be preserved, but she speaks of the main accomplishment with satisfaction.

To find Phelps Mill from Fergus Falls, go east on Fir Av. or northeast on Friberg into County Road 1. Follow it north and east to County Road 45. There a Phelps sign will direct you a mile northward.

(Geneva Tweten died Nov. 5, 1968, while a candidate for the Minnesota House of Representatives.)

MILLS

Trip No. 21 / Old Mill State Park

OLD MILL STATE PARK, about 350 road miles northwest of Minneapolis, has kind of a funny history.

One Lars Larson Sr. followed his sons to that area in the early 1880s and built the first mill on the Middle River, a tributary of the Snake River, which runs into the Red River.

It was a water-wheel job. Larson built a dam with logs and boards. A head of water caved out the boards. A flood was washing away the building with its machinery when one of the Larsons roped it to a tree.

For his next mill, Lars Sr. turned to the air. He put up some kind of a windmill, and the wind blew it down.

For No. 3, the persistent miller returned to the stream. While he was building another water mill, his son John bought a Case steam engine to power No. 4. The Case (a second-hand purchase) didn't hold steam any too well, and it was replaced by an Ames. Thereafter the Larsons did reasonably well.

The *Sheaf,* a weekly newspaper at Warren, Minn., 18

miles southwest of the park, has put a more detailed history of the mills into a leaflet with photographs and diagrams.

At the Sheaf office I found Edgar Mattson and his son Neil, who publish the *Sheaf* in partnership with Edgar's brother Oliver.

Neil is in the historical society and has compiled a lively account of the whole Old Mill Park development, which is a considerable recreational asset to the area.

Following the Mattsons' instructions, I found the park by striking out on Marshall County Road 3 northeastward where it leaves Hwy. 75 on the north edge of town and following the blacktop for about 17 miles.

"It's a nice community park," Edgar had said, and he was putting it modestly.

There is nothing mossy-looking about its something like 280 acres.

Stretching along the Middle River, which meanders through grassy banks and clumps of leafy trees, are picnic grounds and broad playing fields.

A sandy natural swimming hole runs off into the river. The State Parks Department has outfitted it handsomely with stone bathhouse, dock, ropes and platform.

On a Friday morning I found a group of young people swimming and picnicking by the pool. There was a lifeguard on duty, and more swimmers were arriving, a couple of them in a fancy sports car.

MILLS

Trip No. 22 / Mill on Beaver Creek

YOU CAN DO this one in a day, but two are better. It calls for a leisurely pace — pausing, admiring, taking pictures.

I'm talking about Houston County, in the southeastern corner of Minnesota.

It's about 160 miles south to LaCrescent. The first place I saw for lunch there turned out to be a good one, east side of Hwy. 61. Liver, onions, cole slaw, strawberry pie — all good. Nice-looking motels in the area.

My destination was a place called Sheldon on Beaver Creek, where Owen R. Dickie, a Waterville, Minn., reader had reported a water power mill in operation.

I had charted a course to Reno, Minn. (did you know

we had a "Reno"?), west to Caledonia, and northwest to Sheldon.

The hills along the Mississippi River bank are never steeper and prettier than they are south of LaCrescent. The road west from Reno was under repair. People farther south advised me to go on down to New Albin, Iowa, just across the border, and then turn back northwest along the gravel road which follows Winnebago Creek. Excellent advice.

It's a country creek with little secluded-looking farms along its valley. At one place the road goes under a big maple, next to a barn. When I stopped to take a picture of some crazy sandstone banks, a bank swallow poked its head out of a hole right next to my car.

Eventually Houston County Road 5 takes you out of the valley. Then you get some high views following it to Caledonia. Here matters become a little tricky. Go west through town to Hwy. 44, north on 44 beyond the creamery (on the left). Then turn west on Hwy. 76.

This road jogs around a bit, then turns north. About a mile from the corner, at the first crossroad, turn left (west) and you're on your way down the valley into Sheldon. Follow Houston County Road 10 and watch closely. At the bottom of the valley the road will bridge Beaver Creek. Just beyond the bridge a side road bends back sharply to the left. Look back to the left along the creek. You'll see the mill.

It's a three-story building of native stone, built in 1876. When I say native stone, I mean that tan, milky stuff with the beautiful texture. Beaver Creek comes out from underneath it.

Next to it is a long stone barn, nearly as old as the mill, and beyond is a bridge and a grassy walk, flanked by arborvitae hedges, to a neat white frame house. Mr. and Mrs. Ivan L. Krugmire live here with their two children, Elaine and Edward.

Krugmire, a quiet, friendly man, obligingly took me back to the mill, threw it in gear, and for the first time in my life I saw belts flying and wheels spinning in a direct water-to-grinder hook-up.

Krugmire uses the mills strictly for feed-grinding. It once made Schech's Best flour. It was built by one John Blinn and sold to M. J. Schech, Mrs. Krugmire's grandfather. Her father, Ed, ran the mill until his death in 1941.

The Krugmires decided they would like to try farming in 1945 and have been doing a good job of it. Both their children are 4-H'ers, and their white ducks, on the millpond, took first prize at the Houston County Fair.

Krugmire said he doesn't run the mill for everybody, but he's used to people coming in the road to look at it and doesn't mind. "They're always taking pictures of it," he said.

The town of Sheldon, a short way west, consists of one very small store. Here I took Houston County Road 11 to the left, turned right on Houston County Road 4 and followed this north. Hwy. 16 back to LaCrescent was closed for repairs, so I took Hwy. 76 north to Winona.

MILLS

Trip No. 23 / Fairhaven on Clearwater River

A WOMAN WALKED up to me at the State Fair and asked why I hadn't taken more tours around Annandale. She mentioned a little place called Fairhaven near there. She said it had an old millpond and a dam.

Herewith my report:

I went out Hwy. 12 to Cokato, then turned north at the co-op creamery on Wright County Road 3. Hwy. 12 isn't much along that section, but once you get on the county road, the curvy ups and downs and engaging countryside should begin to rebuild your attitude.

Just across the Crow River (North Fork) I saw a "Riverside Cemetery" sign and took an impulsive turn to the right. Another sign and another right turn brought me to an interesting spruce-bordered cemetery with names like Sikkila, Sarenpa, Bukkila, Hoikka, Sirnio, Hokkanen, Karpinen, Kallunki, Saksa, Ulku, Lantto and Lappi.

Back on the county road and three miles farther north,

I admired a view with a pond below to the right and a blue-roofed barn to the left.

At Hwy. 55 turn left into South Haven, north to Fairhaven and left to a little crossroads place. Here Sherrill Smith, owner of the Duck Inn, directed me to the "mill dam."

"Straight ahead to the church (Concordia Evangelical

Lutheran) and down the hill to the left." Once down the hill take the fork to the right. Shortly you will come to an old weathered building with a loading platform roof which has half collapsed. There are holes in the floor and stair boards missing, if you look inside.

It's an old feed mill and the first item in a photographer's paradise. For students of texture I recommend the deteriorating shakes on its sides. You'll find it reflected in a stagnant, algae-spotted pond on the lower side.

Beyond it the Clearwater River rushes over a cracking concrete dam, and beyond that interlace the branches of heavy-trunked willows. If this isn't enough to photograph, there are half-sunken rowboats and a variety of elevations, accessible by foot paths, from which to shoot the scene.

I ducked in again on the way out of Fairhaven. Proprietor Smith said that Bill Seutter rented boats on the pond and considerable ice fishing went on throughout the winter. When I asked about the mill owners, he referred me to Mrs. Carrie Noyes, 84, who lived down the road by a creek.

I found her walking through the grass at her white frame house, and when I asked if she was Mrs. Noyes, she said, "What's left of her."

The dam had been replaced a number of times, she said. "When I was a little girl, we children used to stand below it and let the water hit us. Weren't we darned fools?"

A Grant Graham had owned the dam and operated the mill, she said, and when he died his wife sold it to a non-Fairhaven resident, and the property has been in the hands of one nonresident or another ever since.

On the way out I recalled that Smith had mentioned talk about making a state park of the 17 acres around the millpond and I resolved to check on it. When I did, state park officials told me that the area is too small for a state park but that they know the place, consider it a beauty spot, and feel that it would be ideal for a county park.

Returning to the cities, I took in Annandale, a pleasant town on Pleasant Lake, which has a public access.

MILLS
Trip No. 24 / Seppman Mill (Wind)

THE WAY TO meet the mood of late fall and approaching winter is head-on. One should have things like a fireplace and a warm bed and a snug house for contrast, of course.

But the lethargic contentment of the fireside should be interlarded with long drafts of fresh air, sallies into the teeth of the gale, hill-climbing and views at the top of wild-armed trees and desolate, forlorn, deserted structures where summer was locked in the root cellar and left to starve eons ago.

Without all this how can one appreciate the fireside?

There are dozens of desolate hilltops, and finding one's own and keeping it secret truly enhances its desolation, so I shall name only one, as an example.

It is about 1½ miles northwest of Minneopa State Park. You can build a fire and roast a wiener and enjoy the waterfalls and paths around the park. This is preliminary, to prepare you for the contrast.

Now notice, if you will, a side road across the high-way (old Hwy. 60) from the park entrance and a little north of it. That road leads straight up and down a hill to Hwy. 68. Turn left.

Drive out 68 about 1¼ mile. Here is a roadside parking area. It has a "plaque," that is, a legend in black letters on a white background. It says:

"Seppman Mill. One of the first stone grist mills in Minnesota. Built in the European style by Louis Seppman and Herman Hegley in 1864. The stone for the mill was hauled from Seppman's pastures and hardwood for interior fittings came from the surrounding forests."

Now observe (of course you already have, but take a good look) at the structure atop the hill across the gully behind the parking area. It is what is left of the Seppman mill, and it is truly a forlorn sight.

Except for a few scraggly tree branches there is nothing to interrupt your vision. The wind-driven Dutchmill propellers which once turned the stone that ground the grist are gone. The windows are open and black as the inside of the whale that swallowed Jonah.

The stucco-like layer of cement has peeled here and there to reveal the sturdy stone walls which may catch, if the sun is shining, the crooked shadow-lines cast by the branches just as they have been frozen by approaching winter in the middle of their demented gestures.

If you want to jog into the gully, duck under the rusty barbed wire, cross the ditch and climb through the beggar's lice and dry weeds to take a look inside the old mill, further desolation awaits you — the pock-marked stones, heavy enough to smash an automobile — the decaying hardwood workings in a forlorn pile on the floor. That's all.

MILLS
Trip No. 25 / Fugle's Mill on the Root

YOU CAN HIT the antique hunting trail in almost any direction as the craze grows.

Men can be as nutty about antiques as can their wives, but if they aren't, a good answer for the wives might be a place called Fugle's Mill, southeast of Rochester, Minn.

At Fugle's there's plenty of a mechanical nature to interest the men. All of the workings, in fact, are of a real old-time flour mill whose three sets of huge stone grinders and an elaborate refining mechanism were driven by power from the Root River (North Fork) back in 1868 when Matthew Fugle built it with an ingenious know-how brought from Germany.

The old stone building stands about as solidly as ever on the banks of the Root, where Fugle's bridge-building grandson, Joe Chase and wife, stand ready to show the visitors through the premises for a small fee and trace for you the transfer of water power through axles, mammoth gears of oak and steel, belts, drivewheels, endless-chain hoists and, finally, revolving drums once enclosed in fine silk through which the flour was sifted.

I missed the way at Rochester on a detour around some superhighway construction and wound up on Olmsted County Road D. Realizing I was lost, I stopped at a place called "Mayowood Greenhouse, Gallery and Antiques."

There was a young man working in the garden outside the front door of the greenhouse-gallery who knew all about Fugle's, told me how to get there and drew me a map. "My grandfather used to go there on picnics," he said. "While you're here you might as well look around," he said, and showed me his antiques, some chairs from Italy, a fireplace from France and a lot more while his wife and toddler danced in another room to some bouncy phonograph music.

"This rock garden was in the greenhouse so we kept it," he said. "My grandfather built this greenhouse. My grandfather was Dr. Will Mayo. I'm Ned Mayo. We opened this place last spring."

"How did you get on this track?" I asked. "How did you develop an interest in antiques?"

"Well, mainly from what I took up in school, I guess —art and archaeology."

Following his concise instruction, I found the mill without any further trouble. Joe Chase was out building bridges, but his wife, a cheery woman with animated eyes, showed me not only the mill's machinery but a collection of at least a thousand and one antiques, curios and oddments.

They stood on three floors of the mill and even outside. There was a turntable around which a horse once circled to power a sorghum mill. "I watched this work when I was a little girl," she said, "and I never could understand how the horse could remember just when to lift her hind feet to step over the revolving rod. She couldn't see back there, but she always lifted her hind feet at just the right time."

Mrs. Chase showed the enthusiasm and affection for antiquity which makes such viewing a pleasure and told me where to turn (at Simpson) on the way back, so as to take Olmsted County Road 16 past St. Bridget's Church (stone), built in 1859.

MILLS

Trip No. 26 / Berning's on the Crow

IF YOU HAVE A YEN to skate on a mill pond, as pictured on the old-fashioned calendars, I can tell you where to find one that's suitable after a heavy freeze.

It's on the northwestern edge of Hennepin County, on the wiggly Crow River, about two miles southwest of Hwy. 152.

The kids usually skate there after it's frozen solid.

It's the mill pond of Berning's Mill. Leon Berning runs the mill (it grinds feed and adds vitamin-mineral concentrate for livestock) as did his father and grandfather. His brother Everett runs Berning's Tavern, nearby.

In the tavern Mrs. Everett Berning told me how their boy pulled a staggering catch of northerns out of the river during its high flood stage of 1952.

The dam nearly went out that year. Her husband and brother-in-law Leon Berning got little sleep for five days as they worked to stem the flood. They used sandbags and went out in a boat to cut down trees with a chain saw.

It was the worst flood that their grandfather had seen, and he was 90 when he died in 1959.

On the river side you can see the huge gears and shafts and belted wheels, supported by aged and weathered timbers, where the power is transmitted from the turbine water wheel, in the mill race beneath the surface to the sawmill.

"I'm used to it," Leon said philosophically when I asked whether curious onlookers bothered him.

"Last summer," he recalled, "there were a bunch of painters in the park across the river. Later when I went into the art gallery at the State Fair I saw a big picture of the mill hanging there."

The park to which he referred is Riverside Park on the Hennepin County side of the river (the mill is in Wright County). The Bernings own the park land but lease it to the Sportsmen's Club and the American Legion.

Below the present mill, half in the water, are some gray wooden pilings. "That was the flour mill," Leon said. Its business died for lack of a railroad.

The old flour mill sagged, and it was pulled down a few years ago. Every day during its dismantling Mrs. Everett Berning took a snapshot of it, and she keeps the pictures in the tavern. She hated to see the old building go.

MILLS

Trip No. 27 / Millerville's Working Mill

YOU'LL NEED DIRECTIONS when you get to Millerville, which is a wide place in Douglas County Rd. 7, northwest of Alexandria, Minn.

Just north of the Millerville Supermarket and Hardware, turn right (east), go a mile on gravel to a "Mill" sign, then turn left (north) another mile, and you're there.

A pond reflects trees, rushing water shoots under the road, a mill hulks beyond, to the left, and beyond that stand the miller's farmhouse, outbuildings, Hereford cattle and a black Lab-Chesapeake.

Robert W. Green, the miller, came in from the barn as the dog barked. As we exchanged greetings, the bark subsided, and there stood a friendly dog named Promise. The name, Green said, was to remind their children— Dawn, Dana, and Denise—of a promise. ("If we get you the dog, promise you'll take care of it.")

Geese ambled across the road—tame white ones and black-and-white-faced Canadians—from mill to lake. The Canadians flew in, spent some time watching the others and then joined them, Green said.

Asked if the millpond-lake has a name, he said, "When I bought the place (270 acres), I was told that the lake's name is whatever my wife's first name is." By that rule, it is now Lake Pamela. It had been Lake Helen. The water is an upper reach of Minnesota's Chippewa River,

which wends its way south into the Minnesota River.

Green is starting his fifth year here, but he is no stranger to mills. He spent part of his boyhood sweeping out his grandfather Green's mill at Morris, Minn. His father, Leonard Green, had the Farmers Elevator at Kensington, Minn. Bob Green worked for his father, struck out for Portland, Ore., where he drove double-bottom trucks (cement, fertilizer and such), and all the

while he and Pamela had their eyes on the old Millerville Mill, founded in 1873 by F. G. Dobmeyer, then sold to George DeLeeuw, who was about ready for retirement.

"Tell us when you're ready to sell," the Greens told the DeLeeuws. The DeLeeuws drove out to Oregon to tell them, and the Greens bought the mill, the farm and the portable milling equipment that went with it.

During their first year back in Minnesota, Green taught a course in truck driving at Alexandria Vo-Tech. After that he was too busy.

The truck-hauled portable mill covers a wide territory (20 miles in different directions). Green cleans grain, dries corn and grinds grain on the road and also does a lot of stationary feed grinding (no flour any more) back at the old mill. He also sells power "choring" equipment (barn cleaners, silo unloaders, cattle feeders, swinging stackers and such things as Armadixon—iron for baby pigs).

A power mainstay in the old mill is the Fairbanks-Morse one-lunger cited in the "Douglas County Area Guide." One-lunger means one cylinder. It stands upright something like the boiler on a stationary steam engine. The piston weighs 500 pounds, the wrist pin 98. The engine is a diesel. Its exhaust descends straight into a pit, from which it is piped into another pit, from which it runs straight through the roof.

"If it didn't run that way, you'd hear it all over the county," Green said.

The big antique runs 15 hours daily through the winter. "I run a generator with it now," said its master. "There used to be a belt running up from here. I overhauled the machine awhile back. Parts are no problem; they're still making them."

Each day the one-lunger goes into action on compressed air. Said Green:

"I get up 250-270 pounds of air pressure to get her rolling. Get her to coasting, and then away she goes. I've got a compressor up here to keep up the pressure for the next start.

"In winter this water is hot under here, It picks up the heat when cooling the engine, and then it warms up the engine in the morning.

"Most diesels will burn about five gallons an hour; I don't think you could burn over a gallon an hour with this one. If you pull her pretty hard, she'll smoke, but otherwise there's no smoke at all. Burns clean and uses less fuel than a diesel truck."

He pointed out some smaller diesels in the engine room. "These are all, you might say, antiques. This is my small one. At one time it produced current for a whole town in South Dakota. I use them all."

History of Millerville, published in 1930, tells how Dobmeyer used water power in the beginning. The water went through a turbine. The mill ground flour between stones. Roller mills were installed in 1907. A steam engine replaced water power, and diesel power replaced steam.

There's always work to be done.

"Farmers probably have only eight to ten days to get their crop in," Green said. "So their grain cleaning has to be done quick. It started late this year. We started cleaning a couple or three weeks ago.

"We take care of a lot of farmers over three weeks, grinding feed, going long hours. There are more than a couple dozen. I don't really go too far straight west or east, but north and south—Parkers area, Garfield, Brandon. In the summertime selling helps keep things going. You've got to stay busy, otherwise you get in trouble.

"In winter it's dairy operations, and that's when everybody is really pumping milk. That's our busy time . . . we feed the cows."

Following the road over the earthen dam and a bit east of the mill into the woods we found a log cabin. Mill-founder Dobmeyer built it with hand-hewn hardwood logs chinked with mortar. The old cabin is still in good condition.

MILLS
Trip No. 28 / End of Old Tunnel

A READER, COMMENTING on the various old mills de-scribed in my columns, piqued my curiosity by mention-ing an Old Tunnel Mill about eight miles northeast of Spring Valley, Minn.

I went there. Herewith my report:

Spring Valley is on a main highway (U.S. 63), and the drive there is more or less a breeze. It's about 15 miles north of the Iowa line and takes about 2½ hours to get there. The state scenic wayside a few blocks east of Hwy. 52 at Oronoco occupies a pleasant spot on the Zumbro River (southern branch). It's about two-thirds of the way to Spring Valley.

Once in Spring Valley and having no road directions to the Old Tunnel Mill, I set up headquarters in a place called The Coffee Shop by ordering tuna fish, Chinese style, which turned out to be tuna fish chow mein.

My waitress never heard of the mill.

"You never heard of the tunnel mill?" asked another

waitress. "Every Girl Scout should have heard of it."

"Every girl should have heard of it," said another.

Mrs. Harold Bronlow, co-owner of the place with Mrs. Roy Nelson, advised me to head north on Hwy. 74. "If you get lost, you won't mind. It's kind of pretty."

The Old Tunnel Mill turned out to be in use as a barn

and not suitable for public viewing. I found it by following State Hwy. 74 (gravel) northward 6½ miles to a crossroad, going west 1½ miles to a "T" and then north another mile. It was a tall, wide-eaved red building in a farmyard, its windows broken, its outer stairs askew. Nobody was home, and some barking dogs discouraged my searching around for the tunnel which once brought water through the hill to the mill. However, I did not regret my mission. Mrs. Bronlow had been right. It was pretty back there.

At one point, where Hwy. 74 dips to the bottom of the Root River valley, I saw what I think is the sheerest stretch of vertical sandstone cliff that I have seen in the state. So sheltering is it that the Root River along its base usually, I imagine, is as smoothly reflecting as when I saw it — except when it is in flood, and the bent condition of the shrubbery attested that it often is.

Big white oaks and elms surrounded a little pavillion near the cliff, and a sign labeled the area Mason Park. So near to the wall-like cliff is it that noises like the slam of a car door have a hollow sound, as if one were inside a huge armory.

CHAPTER V   PARKS

Trip No. 29 / Taylors & St. Croix Falls

LATE IN MAY the season gets into full swing at one of the Upper Midwest's most popular park areas, the Interstate Parks on both sides of the St. Croix River at Taylors Falls, Minn., and St. Croix Falls, Wis.

On the Wisconsin side the park's official title is "Trap Rock Interstate Park" — on the Minnesota side, simply "Interstate Park."

As the season progresses, things get better and better. The trees leaf and pretty soon the bluebells sprout from the cracks in the dark rock.

This is the seventy-third year that the Taylor Falls excursion boatrides have been in operation. Carl C. Muller started them in 1906. His son, Bob, and Bob's son-in-law, Dennis Raedeke, still are adding to the fleet.

Camping is as popular as the boats. Each year Minnesota and Wisconsin add more campsites to their parks on both sides of the river, but each year the demand seems to be about double the supply.

Nor is there any dearth of one-day picnics. In the spring there always seems to be a group of school picnickers hiking and scrambling around. Later the only thing that changes is the median age.

I found some junior high girls coming down a steep rock face and took their pictures. "Does your teacher know you're climbing rocks?" I asked one.

She admitted not.

"It's against the rules," a friend on the flat volunteered. She got out a list of rules and showed it to the climber, who was down by then.

She read it. "Gee, that's right. It says no rock climbing."

One boy insisted on calling to me across the river, "Hey, mister, what time is it?"

*　　　　*　　　　*　　　　*

The excursion boats run continuously over the weekend. Their pilots scarcely get time to eat lunch.

Canoe rentals usually keep all the canoes busy. I found Raedeke at a dockside phone taking reservations. "I can't promise that many four-man canoes. Some of you might have to split up."

Memorial Day sees something like 10,000 visitors swarming over the Interstate Park rocks on opposite sides of the St. Croix, spilling through woodland walking trails, paddling canoes, lolling in sunny spots, rubbernecking in excursion boats, launching runabouts, eating, playing and in general making the most of the fair weather.

From high hiking trails along the sheer rock dropoffs of the Wisconsin side, one gets a grandstand view of his fellow celebrators across the river gorge winding between the railings lining the deep rock potholes on the Minnesota side.

From the Minnesota side, from the Taylors Falls Boat Co. canoe and excursion docks, from its festive boats, or from rock ledges, one gets an opposite view of his fellow humans lining the rock walls and sand beaches of Wisconsin and looking back at him.

"I thought you promised to watch Marilyn," I heard a picnicking mother reprove her 10-year-old son.

"I thought Cathy was watching her," he said. Meanwhile:

"Hello, little birdie," said a 17-year-old boy shuffling along a ledge toward a nest while three girls watched and giggled. Meanwhile:

"Let's drop a few pebbles on him," suggested an envious youngster to his fellows as a kid raced his high-powered fiberglass watersled below the cliff where they sat.

Others ran among the trees, bounced orange volley-balls over nets, or played badminton, kittenball, or catch. Some ate fried chicken at the picnic tables on the flats near the water level. A few just sat silently, usually by the water, looking across it, up it, down it. A boy sat on a stump doing that—just looking. "My dad was in the canoe races," he said, "He didn't win, though. The bow kept slipping."

PARKS

Trip No. 30 / Games in Parks

ALTHOUGH FISHING IS popular everywhere, it yields from time to time to quite a variety of things to do in our scenic parks and campgrounds. Nearly all our state parks, of course, have hiking trails (with printed charts as aids in appreciating nature) but people, left to their ingenuity, have some additional ideas.

For example, at William O'Brien State Park north of Marine-on-St. Croix, I came upon a group of girls swarming around one of their number who was clutching a brown paper bag. The girls turned out to be part of an outing of Friendly Valley Junior Girl Scouts from Bayport, Stillwater and Marine. The girl with the paper bag had found it in a hollow tree. It was the prize in a treasure hunt. It was full of candy bars.

Farther upstream, in the campground at Interstate

Park, husbands and wives together were playing a game of "Jarts." Two couples had parked their camping trailers and had done some fishing without much luck, but that didn't keep them from having fun. "Jarts" is something like horseshoes played with darts. You toss them under-handed and try to get them to land in a hoop laid on the ground, and that's what these couples were doing while the St. Croix rolled by them in the background.

In another corner of the camp two boys also had given up on fishing and were having a contest throwing kitchen knives at a cedar pole.

Another notch up the river there was another game under way — the dating game. Sitting on a rock, a Macalester College couple admired the scenery. The girl, a freshman in art, was getting a lot of free information. Her date was a junior in geology and had been telling her about the volcanic rocks around the Taylors Falls Dalles. Four other Macalester students, fresh from a rented canoe ride, dangled their feet over the wall by the excursion boat dock.

*　　　*　　　*　　　*

Baker Park in Hennepin County has big resources not only for camping but more extroverted, athletic action.

Driving into Baker with its ¾-mile shoreline on Lake Independence 2 miles north of Maple Plain, one can see, by swiveling one's neck, three kittenball games in progress across a grassy valley, picnickers eating at tables on the shady slopes facing the lake, any number of volley ball and smaller games, kids on the playground equipment, swimmers in the water and speedboats on it.

One sunny afternoon at Baker Park I saw:

Old folks in wheel chairs admired the lake while kids from 3 on up exercised on a jungle gym. Among them, two were too small to give their names.

An electroplating foreman gave rides in his motor-boat to youngsters on a company picnic. He carried some of them aboard.

An Edina couple had the smallest picnic going—just the two of them near the water's edge.

Of all the picnickers, the tiredest were the mothers escorting youngsters from the cold drink coolers to the bathroom up on the hill.

PARKS
Trip No. 31 / Covered Bridge Park

SOUTHERN MINNESOTA WAS settled earlier than the northern part of the state, and its nineteenth century way of life was more akin to that of agricultural areas to the east.

The appeal of this picturesque New England-like phase of its past and the wisdom of preserving it is beginning to soak in among the citizenry to the south.

The natives like the idea and the tourists like it. It might even be the key to an era when Minnesota's southerners can compete for tourists on an equal footing with its northerners.

Evidence of the south's awakening to its historic advantages now claims public notice at Zumbrota, Minn.

Zumbrota, of course, is on the Zumbro, one of many startlingly pretty (especially in autumn) streams which wander eastward through grassy meadows, cedar-dotted

banks, rich foliage and cut rock to the Mississippi.

The awakening is now arriving via what is called the Zumbrota Covered Bridge Society.

Zumbrota has one of the few nineteenth century covered bridges remaining in their original condition. It's probably the only one in the state.

Hence, Covered Bridge Park, a charming project, is off to an interesting existence.

The bridge is a magnet which draws other nostalgic

items to the park such as a Civil War log cabin from the Truman Skaaro farm near Nerstrand, Minn., a 105-year-old country schoolhouse from Belvidere, a fancy lamp-post from the bridge that replaced the covered bridge in Zumbrota, and the first Milwaukee Road workmen's out-house in this area.

For park purposes the latter has been converted to a toolshed, inasmuch as a modern restroom with city plumbing and showers for campers has been installed.

PARKS
Trip No. 32 / Frontenac Trail

How ARE YOUR climbing legs? The climbingest trail that I have found in any of Minnesota's state parks will answer that.

It's in a section of Frontenac State Park overlooking Lake Pepin. This new section is northeast of Hwy. 61 and you reach it by turning off 61 at the "Old Fronte-nac" sign about 10 miles below Red Wing.

A good strip of blacktop will take you off the Old Frontenac road. Turning left, at a state park sign, it leads you up a long grade and around to the right where you reach a bare hilltop. Trees, mostly oaks, fringe a high bluff facing the Lake Pepin part of the Mississippi River.

A permanent building stands on the plateau. There are picnic tables, a parking area, and out-houses.

If you want climbing exercise, look for a knee-high sign reading "Trail" by the trees at the top of the bank.

This bank is 400 feet above the water. You'll find an innocent looking path leading over the edge by the sign.

The darned thing takes a switchback zig-zag course clear down the thickly wooded bank to the bottom of its 400-foot vertical rise and the shore of Lake Pepin.

The Division of State Parks has been interested in the Frontenac area since 1935, but the park didn't get established until 1957, and land still is being acquired. The state owns 1,000 of 2,600 hoped-for acres.

The high bluff described above is for picnicking and camping. The Indians called it "Point No Point." The name's negative flavor can be attributed to the Indians' experience while paddling up Lake Pepin. The bluff can be seen for a long time without seeming to get any closer.

Among the bluff's points of interest is a rock with a hole big enough to ride a horse through, if you don't mind riding off the cliff. The Indians are supposed to have used this for some kind of riding test — I can't imagine how.

Red Wing citizens have been working for a long time to help the park develop. They have donated land and raised funds for the purchase of other land, including woods in which stands a beautiful stone house called "Bramble Hall" by Mabey, Alice and Nellie Moore, its former owners.

PARKS

Trip No. 33 / Whitewater

ONE OF MINNESOTA's prettiest state parks, Whitewater, takes in something like $45,000 during a good year, for entry stickers, camping fees, cabin rentals and green fees on its nine-hole golf course cozily hugging its green valley bottom.

Minnesota's state parks pay about 60 per cent of their way, but parks like Whitewater have a higher pay-off.

Hiking trails around Whitewater's sandstone hills, its small but picturesque river, its golf course and swimming

pool have made it a prime southern Minnesota attraction. Its riverbank campgrounds are usually full, and you have to get your cabin reservations early.

The park will be especially pretty in the fall, and so will the drive from Weaver, Minn., through the park to St. Charles, Minn., on Hwy. 74, or the other way if you prefer. St. Charles is about 20 miles east of Rochester on Hwy. 14.

*　　　*　　　*　　　*

St. Croix State Park: It's a long, long trail awinding to the "Kettle River Vista" in this park with its 21 miles of frontage on the St. Croix River.

This is one of the wildest and most thickly grown of the Minnesota parks, and it's quite flat. If you're a long-view scenery lover, it may give you claustrophobia.

The 10-mile gravel road to the Kettle River at the south end of the park is often a tunnel of verdure. This, however, has its compensations for close-up nature lovers.

The verdure consists mostly of second-growth pine, spruce and hardwoods interspersed with open meadows —ideal conditions for deer. Popping out of the woods onto a bridge crossing one of several streams, I happened upon two deer standing in the water. They stayed there while I took a picture from the car window.

The turning leaves should make this quite a trip in the fall.

The park's long suits are picnicking, nature study, stream fishing and hiking. It has swimming, 50 camp-sites, 10 housekeeping cabins, and rental boats. Saturday evenings there are nature science movies at the "council ring," a small outdoor semi-circle of benches near one of the camp headquarters buildings where you can buy groceries, curios, pop or whatever. The services are slanted for the campers.

To find the park, drive east out of Hinckley on Hwy. 48. An interesting return trip is to continue on 48 east to Danbury, Wis., south on Hwy. 35 to Hwy. 8 and then west to Minneapolis.

PARKS
Trip No. 34 / Wirth's Wild Flowers

A NATURE LOVER'S summer isn't complete around Minneapolis unless he has paid at least one visit to the Eloise Butler Wild Flower Garden in Theodore Wirth Park.

One's knowledge of the blooms can advance over the years if one manages to check out the garden during a different month each year — August for the Wild Daisies, Blazing Star, Bee Balm, Monkshood — September for the Downy Gentian, Prairie Aster, Goldenrod, Red Turtlehead, Woods Aster — October for the fall foliage, the Witch Hazel, the Rattlesnake-root, and so on.

The aforenamed are a small fraction of the varieties scattered through the secluded 13 acres, of course. Posted at the office building near the entrance you'll find a detailed list for the month, running into a hundred or so.

The garden is a mercifully quiet place. The viewers are confined to narrow pathways lined by white cords to mark the way. There are no playgrounds within the sanctuary. Domestic animals are kept out.

Viewing the flowers is a quiet, even introspective occupation. Forgotten kinds bring recollections of early childhood. So does the close, minute inspection which their identification requires.

Most of the blooms are small, inconspicuous, the opposite of showy, the sort of things that we forget to examine after childhood with its infinite leisure has gone.

The garden closes at 6 p.m. I entered at 4:40 p.m. on a Friday. It was so quiet that I had the illusion of hearing every individual bird and chipmunk in the place. Birds were working on a bird feeder suspended by the office.

The woodland or lower part of the garden is in a hollow, and as the sun descended a bit, the shadows outnumbered the sunny patches, and then a tall yellow daisy, caught in the sunlight, sprang vividly alive against a dark piny background.

This, I learned from a handy plaque, is "Wild Golden-glow" (Rudbeckia Laciniata).

Climbing the path to the upper or prairie garden, I was met by a deliciously subtle fragrance, better than My Sin, better than Grandma's hot apple pie, and the name on the plaque was better still — "Bouncing Bet," white, lavender and tantalizing.

Once I was lucky enough to hook up with a ladies' garden club tour guided by Kenneth E. Avery, the Wild Flower Garden curator.

His remarks were informative, frank and to the point.

"This is the purple trillium," he said, "otherwise known as stinking Benjamin. The odor isn't strong, but there is a faint suggestion of men's locker room about it."

Farther down the path he pointed out the "interrupted fern," which gets its name from two flat green things among the fronds along the stem. "These two never grow any larger," he said. "Hence, 'interrupted.' They are a specialized part of the producing spores."

"Are they the sex organs?" asked one of the ladies who believed in calling a spade a spade.

"That's almost it," he agreed. He went on to explain the spores' system of reproduction. "There are so many of them, because to take root two of them must just happen to fall together where growing conditions are ideal. Unless there are two, you don't have the right number of chromosomes."

After pointing out some "tooth worts," maple blooms and several other phenomena, he let the ladies proceed on their own and headed for other duties. I stopped him long enough to get an estimate on attendance.

"Nobody really knows," he said. "There are two gates, and we don't get an accurate count. Last season's estimate was 100,000, and I don't think it was too far off."

It would be better, he said, if some of the visitors didn't come at all. A lot of them expect to find a cultivated garden. They are disappointed in the unraked wildness of the precious 13 acres in Avery's care. "They go walking through, and they don't really see anything."

If you look sharp you may see Large Trillium, Jack-in-the-Pulpit, Dutchman's Breeches, Virginia Bluebells, Blue Anemone, Bird's-foot Violet, Columbine and Lupine, Lady's Slippers, Rhododendron, Azaleas, Showy Orchis, Wild Blue Indigo, Golden Alexander, Beard-tongue and more.

PARKS

Trip No. 35 / Beaver Creek

HOUSTON COUNTY IN southeasternmost Minnesota deserves attention that it doesn't usually get.

It may be fairly well known that its Root River is beautiful, but seldom has anybody heard of its Winnebago Creek. Everybody should have.

Beaver Creek, a bit north of Winnebago Creek, is better known, but only lately has Beaver Creek Valley State Park begun to catch on with campers, most of whom are from Rochester, Minn.

One reason why so few know Winnebago Creek is its remoteness. It is best followed by taking a little blacktop road that runs northwest out of New Albin, Iowa, and becomes Houston County Road 5 (to Caledonia, Minn.).

For an extra kick I drove down the Wisconsin side of the Mississippi from LaCrosse to De Soto on Hwy. 35 (right by Goose Island County Park) through De Soto to the bridge 3 miles south, across the Mississippi to Lansing, Iowa, and north on Hwy. 182 to New Albin. Lansing has a bit of the old rivertown charm.

North of Lansing on Hwy. 182, two girls and two women sat on an A-frame cabin porch above the highway and looked at the wide, meandering foliage-dotted river.

Once you hit the winding ups and downs along Winnebago Creek to Caledonia, you're in for a lot of fun. You pass close to a number of valley farms. Near one the road goes under big maple tops. In autumn these same maples are flaming red.

Half way to Caledonia I encountered a mother, son and daughter who had pulled two trout out of the creek and were happily heading for their Caledonia home.

To reach Beaver Creek Valley State Park from Caledonia go west across Hwy. 44 and stay on Hwy. 76 until you come to the park sign.

Beaver Creek originates at a spring in the 900-acre park. It has wilderness and modern campgrounds, 1½ miles of trout stream (fishing licenses are sold in the park), seven miles of nature trails, picnic ground, picnic shelter and refectory.

Bluffs line the valley. Park signs warn hikers not to get too close to the edge of cliffs and to be on the alert for rattlesnakes. They are seldom seen, but they are a possibility.

People find fawns and think they were abandoned, or they say that they thought so. The game wardens have to see that they are returned to the forest.

On Houston County Road 10 (after having lost myself, I'll have to confess) I ran onto Schech's Water Power Mill, one of the few old-style mills still operable. It's open to visitors for a fee. The mill is on Beaver Creek north of the park near Sheldon.

CHAPTER VI   RIVER TOWNS

Trip No. 36 / Red Wing

RED WING, MINN., abounds in high views. One of them is from Oakwood Cemetery and another is from Skyline Park.

"Until the Morning Break and the Shadows Fade Away" reads the stone legend to the right as one enters Oakwood. And to the left: "The Memorial Gift of Elijah H. Blodgett to the City of Red Wing."

Blodgett gave the city of Red Wing a splendid gift, indeed. The entry up a long sylvan incline brings one out on a cemetery hill fringed with lacy birches. Looking through them, one sees houses, lawns, streets, trees and buildings spread among the protective neighboring hills — a capsule view of life until the morning break.

Down the hill and through town to another hill, west of southbound Hwy. 61, waits a broader and longer view of the river valley. This is Skyline Park, reached by driving back along the old highway, now running parallel with the new divided highway, and turning uphill through a masonry gateway. Skyline sprawls out between two sections, one open and the other secluded, tucked among stone outcroppings and trees.

Skyline offers a good look at the Mississippi Valley. At high-water stage you will see water in some places where it usually isn't.

Red Wing gives its citizens access to the waterfront, wide acreage, and broad views of the river valley, via public parks, far beyond others so fortunately situated.

The variety of waterfront activity on just an ordinary day (fishing, watercolor paintings, picnicking and watching the river barges go by) shows how the parks are used and appreciated.

The city's newest park "kick" is tree and plant identification. Red Wing is starting to educate nature lovers. It may even educate others who think that parks are for hot dogs and mumblety peg.

The idea is to tantalize one with the mystery of plant biology. The key to the mystery is found in a large stout green-printed sheet of white paper entitled, "Discovery Walks in Red Wing Parks."

On one side are bold schematic maps of Mt. LaGrange (Barn Bluff), Colvill Park, John Rich Park, Central Park and Pierce Park on the Levee. Scattered over each map are numbers. Turn the sheet and you find, after the numbers, names of trees or plants and over the numbers, pictures of the identifying leaves. By combining locations on the map and clues on the leaf chart, you can wander around the parks and come out able to tell Evening Primrose from Sheep Sorrel, Stinging Nettles from Burdock, or Solomon's Seal from Poison Ivy.

It is only fair to note that the prickly, stinging, and poison things are on the wild perimeters.

The Red Wing Art Association prepared the chart-maps, and the Red Wing Lions Club financed their printing. They are available at the Red Wing City Hall, the Chamber of Commerce office, and the Colvill Park concession stand.

Of course, in the parks you can get other things — the broad riverscape view from Scenic Drive Memorial, waterside views at Colvill or Pierce, or a fountainside view of a beautiful church at John Rich.

RIVER TOWNS

Trip No. 37 / Lake City and La Crosse

THE JUNE RAINS came just in time to ward off drought and bring out the verdure in all its emerald splendor.

In a southeasterly direction, generally neglected at this time of year, I tried a run down the Mississippi River valley to Lake City, Minn., and La Crosse, Wis.

If the weather was misty or hazy, so much the better for taming the sun's rays before they came through my windshield.

While you can't beat a clear view from the many hillcrests, neither can you beat a little romantic enchantment on a hot day. A little vapor in the air makes the Mississippi, wide and island-dotted below Lake Pepin, look like a Japanese water color.

On the way down Hwy. 61 on the Minnesota side, I found, as usual, a lot of activity around Lake City on Lake Pepin.

Minnesota's biggest fishing barge is a Lake City pontoon dock in Lake Pepin (a wide part of the Mississippi River).

The barge offers 400 linear feet of outside edge from which poles can be extended and lines dropped into the water. It sports lamplights on regular street-style lamp posts, and it attracts anglers from everywhere, but especially southern Minnesota.

They line its edges all summer and when fall comes, they don warm jackets and mackinaws and keep right at it. The quiet social atmosphere of the dock is not unlike that of a pier at Long Beach, Calif., except that there is more of an internal security about it.

I found people catching crappies off the barge and off the breakwater. On shore a family had a picnic lunch off the hood of their car where it was parked overlooking the water.

Lake City's big marina and trailer park, municipally run, has been refashioned. Trucks and dozers have raised it and a huge parking lot by 7 or 8 feet as a flood-preventive measure. A boaters' club and manager's office have been added.

Mike Hull, a metal equipment factory worker who has lived in Lake City two years, told me that the fishing had been good.

"If I didn't like it, I wouldn't be living here," he said. "I pick the town first and then the job."

La Crosse, about 140 miles southeast of the Twin Cities, surrounded by what it calls "coulee country," is a remarkably tourist-worthy recreation center and very much river-oriented.

Coming into town, I put up at an island motel with an artificial swimming pool in the middle and houseboats docked outside my window. The town stands against a backdrop of beautiful green river bluffs.

Driving east through town on Cass St., I saw an American flag on a pole topping the highest bluff of all. I concluded that there must be a park way up there, and I was right.

Crossing the railroad tracks with the Country Club golf course alongside, I found Bliss Road. It led up through the greenery past an "Alpine" roadhouse to Grandad Bluff Park, a promontory 650 feet above the city.

A plaque described it as "one of the few unglaciated areas of North America" (this is also true of places on the Minnesota side in Houston County) and called attention to Bittersweet Hiking Trail among the blackwood, ironwood and burr oaks.

Among books, leaflets and maps which the La Crosse Chamber of Commerce puts out ("Guide to Better Eating," "Recreation Guide to La Crosse," "La Crosse County Camp Sites") is a dandy entitled "Coulee Country Trails." It describes 22 drives ranging from 25 to 150 miles among the hills and dales.

The dictionary describes a "coulee" as "the bed of a stream, even if dry, when deep and having inclined sides."

This is coulee-rich country. While I was looking over the Mount La Crosse ski area (south of town on Hwy. 61 near the Hwy. 35 turn-off), a local farmer put me on a coulee trail of his own—just turn right off Hwy. 14 onto a county road north of the ski area, he said, and

follow it until it takes you back to Hwy. 14 (and 61). It really takes you up and down those "inclined sides."

Through Labor Day two-hour river cruises leave La Crosse daily.

Upper Mississippi Cruises and Holiday Cruises both offer houseboat rentals.

There is camping in Grandad Bluff Park (one night only by permission from City Park Department); Goose Island County Park, 3 miles south of town on Hwy. 35; Veteran's Memorial Park, 9 miles east on Hwy. 16, and Perrot State Park, 15 miles northwest via Hwys. 35 and 93.

RIVER TOWNS

Trip No. 38 / Fountain City

MUCH OF THE fun of an early ride down the river is the promise of the coming season, from the first light green buds to the rich primary colors of the August flowers. And part of it is the sense of adventure and excitement that summer brings to the river and its towns.

These towns have a special elongation because they are wedged between the water and the bank. Many of their houses have little or no front yards.

Sides and back may sport greenery and flowers, but the incline often demands that for access many of the houses front abruptly upon the sidewalks, like stores.

Hence the second floor balcony, which sometimes projects over the sidewalk and serves as a sort of summer porch.

Sometimes these balconies (or porches) are canti-
levered and sometimes they are supported by rows of
pillars. The resulting portico makes a charming passage-

way for the sidewalk passerby, as in Fountain City. If I were a Chamber of Commerce man in any of these river municipalities, I should do all in my power to encourage people to build more porticos and balconies across the sidewalks.

The scarcity of noonday eating places and the preponderance of supper clubs along the river suggest that things swing at night. For the daylight traveler there is a liberal supply of picnic tables in wayside areas and parks.

Merrick Park, north of Fountain City, is a state park and as such exacts a fee admitting a car to all state parks in Wisconsin for the season. Its byways are beautifully blacktopped, however, its picnic areas plentiful, and there are also camp grounds, boat launching facilities and a bathing beach.

RIVER TOWNS
Trip No. 39 / Maiden Rock

MAIDEN ROCK, WIS., is one of the more picturesque small towns along the Wisconsin side of Lake Pepin, primarily because it is cramped against the high bluff tighter than most.

The side streets to the east rise at almost roller-coaster pitch. The homes on the steep hillsides have deep terraces and long stairways.

If you drive around the big lake to enjoy the fall colors, you will drive through Maiden Rock on Wisconsin Hwy. 35. If you miss the sign, you'll know it by the retaining walls which shoot straight up along the highway.

You might wonder how a town happened to get started in such an awkward place for any town to grow.

I found Louis Dwight Trumbull, 88, in a white house so high on the hillside that a car can't make it on a wet day. A retaining wall of rough, venerable flagstone buttressed his handsome yard.

His father, J. D. Trumbull, founded Maiden Rock.

As a young man J. D. Trumbull was a fur trader for the Hudson's Bay Co. Later he managed a Chicago hotel.

Next he managed the Minnesota House and ran a stageline out of Stillwater. Finally, in the course of his travels, he reached the place where Maiden Rock now stands.

He noticed a lot of logs along the shore. "This is a wide point in the lake," explained Dwight. "The channel is on the Minnesota side. When storms hit the log rafts, logs would get away and float across the lake, and nobody would go after them. It was too far."

It looked like an opportunity to J. D. With a partner named Alfred Harris he bought all the land along the river to Rattlesnake Hollow, a mile downstream. They put up a steam-operated saw and shingle mill. Into it went the stray logs. That was in 1854.

Trumbull's partner died, but things went well financially. Trumbull began selling off the land, piece by piece, to people who were ready to open businesses. The first lot went to Horace Richards, who built a boarding house for the mill workers. Blacksmith, harness shop and store followed.

J. D., himself, took on a general mercantile line and started what probably was the first steamboat passenger service covering the towns around Lake Pepin. He also,

said Dwight, put the first sailboat on the lake.

As Dwight grew up he became a fishing, cycling and ice-boating enthusiast.

Ice boating was fast, and snow wasn't too much of a problem. They built two-passenger cockpits and sometimes carried extras on the crossmember. It was great fun.

Try one of Maiden Rock's hillside streets. Continue north and turn right on County Road "A" right after crossing the Rush River. This will take you up the Rush River valley to Hwy. 10, where you may turn left and return to the Twin Cities.

RIVER TOWNS
Trip No. 40 / Bay City

GENTLE JAUNTS: For an easy-going kind of destination, not too far away, try Bay City, Wis.

It's across the Mississippi from Red Wing and four miles downstream.

Bay City has a park on the river's edge. If you drive toward the river, across the tracks and straight ahead past the hardware store, the road will lead you to the right along the river and into the park.

It's not a fancy park — the auto tracks are sandy and can be dusty on a dry day — but it's an easy-going place with its own unpretentious harbor and boat-launching space, and its tall trees, and it does have a charm of its own.

At least it does if you like to find old boats half-buried in the sand along the water's edge to remind you, sadly, of long-forgotten carefree times.

The same road you came in on, if you follow it straight east out of town, across Hwy. 35, will take you up Isabelle Creek valley to Esdale (a church, a lumber mill and a few houses).

Just before you reach Esdale you'll see Wallie Gerdes' Valley Springs trout farm, 2.4 miles from Bay City.

This is an inviting place with ponds on both sides of the road. Huge maples shade the north side, around a pond by the parking space.

Gerdes, an ex-carpenter, has been in this location for years. His trout, all rainbows, graduate in size from tiny little ones to the big fat ones as you follow the ponds strung in a chain from a small white hatching house on the south side of the road.

Take a good look at Gerdes' neat dwelling. He remodeled it from an old wreck of a building. "You should have seen it," he said. "It was a mess."

To beguile an idle moment or two you can look at some cages which he has neatly labeled: "Japanese Deer," "Golden Pheasant," "Blue India Peacock" and "Lady Amherst Pheasant." He sells his trout by trucking them and by letting you fish for a fee (no license required).

*   *   *   *

David Herold, Taylors Falls, and Dennis Raedeke, ski instructor and excursion boat pilot, have found a way to add zest to canoeing around the river below the falls.

With more than a little help from his wife, who did the sewing, Harold fashioned a sail to give maximum height and spread with a short mast.

The sail is made of cotton sheeting (old parachutes are even better). The mast is a stairway handrail, available from lumber yards. Doweling stiffens the sail at top and bottom.

Raedeke rigged a Taylors Falls-made canvas canoe with a block, fastened at the bottom and at gunwale height, for a mast base, and oak sideboards (keels) with a crosspiece easily unscrewed in event of running aground to hold her steady. The rudder is a paddle.

Caution: When a canoe with sail tips, it can't be "righted" in deep water.

RIVER TOWNS
Trip No. 41 / Prescott

COULD PRESCOTT, WIS., be transformed instantly into the mammoth metropolis which its forefathers envisioned, a great many people today would deem it a pity.

I am thinking, in particular, of riverside residents (one Prescott dream house has its balconies overhanging the water), of pleasure boatsmen who bask on decks or on shore where they can better admire their boats snug in their slips at Prescott's marina or its St. Croix Boat Works, of visitors lapping ice cream cones (not ice milk) from Prescott's riverside Galley Cafe, of picnickers in Prescott's high park with the long view at the south edge

of town, of diners in the high-bank Stardust restaurant or the water's-edge Steamboat Inn, of swimmers at Prescott's beach or Washington County's long, free and sandy Point Douglas beach across the bridge, and of all those people everywhere who dislike industrialized waterfronts.

Prescott has its dribs and drabs of industrial water frontage, but they never have grown to swallow a river.

Small thanks to the aforementioned forefathers, who saw Prescott as the future St. Louis of the north.

James Taylor Dunn in *The St. Croix: Midwest Border River* cites a May 1855 article in the Prescott *Paraclete*. It boasted that Prescott had the same advantageous commercial location for the entire Mississippi valley as had St. Louis for the lower—"the only true head of navigation on both the Mississippi and the St. Croix."

The Hudson, Wis., *North Star* called the article "insulting blackguardism," and there were further sharp exchanges, but the arguers might have spared their blood pressures. Their grandiose dreams just didn't work out.

Oliver Gibbs, a Prescott land salesman, took a more promising tack when he got out an 1859 leaflet advertising no "swamps or stagnant pools to poison the air."

Air, sun, water and picturesque views are Prescott's resources today, likewise Point Douglas' across the bridge, where bathers bask on the sand and Lee Broten's Harbor Inn rents out *Waterbug,* a houseboat, during the summer and half a dozen snowmobiles in the winter.

I found a lot of people on the beach picnicking and floating on air mattresses. Later in the day I couldn't count the bathers.

Prescott isn't trying to be St. Louis any more. It seems to enjoy its lot. If its guests get too lethargic lying in deck chairs or on the sandy beach, it puts on a beauty pageant, or a summer festival called Prescott Riverama.

RIVER TOWNS
Trip No. 42 / Hudson and Burkhardt

THERE IS MUCH to engage the eye and the imagination in and around the place where the primary east-west route through the Twin Cities (Hwy. 12 and Interstate 94) crosses the St. Croix River via the Hudson bridge.

Just south of the bridge on the Minnesota side you

can reach the riverfront by turning off the highway and proceeding through the riverside village of Lakeland as close to the bridge as you can get.

You will come out at a water's edge boat livery called "Beanie's" whose small parking area affords a view of the bridge.

Beanie's has been there since 1929 and is run by Laverne F. Miller, the son of William F. Miller, deceased, whose nickname was Beanie.

* * * *

Inside Beanie's you will find posted near the door dozens of snapshots of fishermen and their catches, some of the latter being sturgeon.

Sturgeon are caught with night crawlers and some of them weigh 50 pounds. Miller will point out a fisherman in his snapshot collection who "never failed to get one."

Miller has 21 boats, and even now there are about 15 "die-hards," as he calls them, who will show up Saturdays and Sundays until the freeze-up.

Late fall is the best time of the year to catch sandpike, says Miller. "They don't bite much in the summer." You can fish through the ice for sandpike into February, legally, but Miller doesn't advise it near his place.

The reason is quite simple: "The ice won't be safe."

* * * *

Having had the low view, perhaps you would like the high view.

For this cross the bridge to Wisconsin. Turn right into the Hudson, Wis., exit. Going north up Hudson's main street, turn right again in Coulee Road at the corner by the Texaco station.

This will take you up the hill to Birkmose Park, named after its donor, C. J. Birkmose, and one of the most

attractive small parks in the Upper Midwest, for its view, for the variety of its tree plantings and for its well-kept condition.

The Indian burial mounds along its hilltop rim give it a historic kind of dignity. There are places where you can enjoy the view from your car, if the park isn't too crowded. Otherwise you'll find it worth getting out of the car to see.

Directly below is Hudson, once called Willow River (which runs through it into the St. Croix). Upriver from the present interstate bridge is where "the Battle of the Piles" took place in July 1871.

At that time another bridge was being built with what upriver Stillwater lumbermen considered insufficient clearance. They boarded paddlewheelers, descended on the construction job, pulled out the pilings and sent them floating down the river. A settlement was negotiated.

*　　*　　*　　*

Six miles up the Willow River from Hudson is Burkhardt, a wide place in County Road A which boasts a store, a filling station, and a big old feed mill. Herein and hereabouts lie possibilities fraught with hope and excitement for scenery-hounds, park-fanciers and admirers of old waterpower mills.

Behind the mill, no longer water-powered, is a sheer drop of 70-some feet down a rock cliff to the millpond. Rock pilings for the old water wheel still stand. Power was transmitted from below by belts. There are those who would like to see the mill restored as a museum and part of a park which, they hope, might extend miles downstream.

Through that area the water descends spectacularly between high sandstone walls, over a high power dam and down a series of cascades into a lake or widening of the river, public access to which is reached by driving half a mile north off County Road A at the Hudson Town Hall and a mile to the right at the next turn-off. (See "Willow River at Burkhardt, Wis." under Parks.)

RIVER TOWNS
Trip No. 43 / Stillwater

WEEKENDS, ESPECIALLY ON Sundays, flurries of activity enliven the St. Croix waterfront along the east edge of long, shady and beautiful Lowell Park in Stillwater, Minn.

Its fountain, flowers, grass, tall trees, antique locomotive and especially its duckboat green "pergola" are
recovered from the beating they took from the flood
waters of 1963.

Few cities of this size have a two-block length of
publicly owned, cared-for, thoughtfully appointed, and
tastefully decorated parkland along their choicest stretch
of waterfront.

Not only does the park put Stillwater citizens and the
general public right on the bank of a topnotch recreational asset but, in the words of Stillwater's Park Board
secretary, "It definitely helps business."

The park's cement slab breaker front, stretching most
of its length, gives boaters a tie-up spot which a lot of
them use, especially on weekends, for shopping excur-

sions on Stillwater's nearby main street running parallel with the river.

A new supermarket's parking lot borders on the park north of the bridge. (The city offers free parking space for park visitors along the edge of the park's major portion south of the bridge.)

Some of the boaters live on their boats for a week or two and buy their groceries here.

* * * *

In 1962 the park's pergola and comfort station was in such bad shape from floods and vandalism that it had to be closed. Then the big flood hit it and caved in a wall.

Today it is renovated and tidied up. It functions, thanks to the Stillwater leaders who saw its value to the city at large.

The city hires a caretaker and an assistant to help him keep everything green and growing, tidy and working.

The budget is small, but officials hope to keep on improving the park from year to year.

* * * *

Stillwater is one of several towns in Minnesota which maintain bathing beaches. It owns a sandy beach on the Wisconsin side of the St. Croix, first turn to the right after you cross the bridge going east.

* * * *

The antique locomotive on display in Stillwater's Lowell Park saw its last years of service on a line, no longer running, from Taylors Falls to Grantsburg, Wis. It was built in 1905 and given to Stillwater in 1955 by the Northern Pacific Railway in conjunction with the Minnesota Railroad Fans Association.

RIVER TOWNS
Trip No. 44 / Marine-on-St. Croix

IN 1838 SOME easterners then living at Marine, Ill., got excited about an opportunity to make a bundle in the lumbering business.

By treaty the Sioux and Chippewas had handed over the upper Mississippi and St. Croix River basins to the whites.

The Marine, Ill., men organized a small lumbering company. There were David Hone, Albert H., George B. and Lewis S. Judd (brothers), Orange Walker, (a Vermont tanner), Hiram Berkey (a farmer), Asa S. and James M. Parker (Vermont bricklayers), William B. Dibble, 23, a New Yorker, Sam Burkleo of Delaware, a Dr. Lucius Green and a Joseph Cottrell.

Hone and Lewis Judd got the job of taking a trip up the St. Croix to pick the best site for a sawmill. When they reached the place where Stillwater now is, they left their riverboat, the *Ariel,* and poled a flatboat all the way up to the falls (now Taylors and St. Croix Falls).

Here they found a group building a sawmill, so they doubled back, picked a spot where Marine-on-St. Croix now stands, staked a claim and went back home for the winter.

They might have been better off if they hadn't staked anything. That winter three characters from upstream jumped the claim. Since the claim was on unsurveyed land, and the claim-jumpers built a cabin on it, they

were able to get $300 from the Illinois men, upon their return, for vacating the premises.

Those were 300 big, uninflated dollars, but the Illinois group thought it was worth it. That's how Marine began.

*　*　*　*

Thus (roughly) opens a 55-page illustrated booklet entitled, "Marine Mills: Lumber Village 1838-1888," by James Taylor Dunn, author of *The St. Croix: Midwest Border River* and Minnesota Historical Society librarian.

Dunn, who lives in Marine, donated the booklet to

the Women's Civic Club of Marine. The women, in turn, are selling Dunn's carefully accurate chronicle of the growth of his hometown to help finance the town's museum.

*   *   *   *

This museum, "The Old Stone House Museum at Marine-on-St. Croix," is a little dandy.

It was built of native stone from the river banks in 1872 as a meeting hall. A corner was equipped as a jail cell. The bars are still there. Later it became a weekend Swedish school. Finally, as times changed, it became a storehouse for the power company.

Then the ladies reclaimed it and began fixing it up as a museum. The curio and antique donors were enthusiastic, but good sense went into choosing the displays.

There are no confusing heaps of thingamajigs. It's easy to concentrate on pertinent items of interest — an old kerosene street lamp, from early Marine Mills, a communion set from an extinct local church, a river log bearing the brand of the town's lumbering founders.

Mrs. Olga Zimmer, who attended the Swedish School, showed me parts of an old-fashioned Swedish kitchen set up in the back room — a bundle of little sticks used as an egg beater and stirrer, a cornbread mold, flour barrel and so on.

Occupying the museum's place of honor is a portrait photograph of Orange Walker, one-time Vermont tanner and the only one of the original lumber company partners who stayed in the company to the very end.

The Stone House Museum is open from 2 to 5 p.m. Saturdays and Sundays. To find it turn west off Hwy. 95 at the center of town, drive uphill and turn right for half a block just before reaching the church.

CHAPTER VII
SMALL MUSEUMS

Trip No. 45 / Gibbs Farm

WELFARE WORK WAS informal 133 years ago.

When little Janie DeBow was 6, her mother fainted, fractured her skull and had to be taken off to the hospital.

Janie, her brother and four sisters had to be farmed out among friends and relatives. Janie went to the Vedders across the meadow from the DeBow house by the creek near East Bethany, N. Y.

Janie kept running back to her empty home and Mrs. Vedder had to leave soapmaking to chase the child, so when the Rev. Jedediah Stevens, his wife and family passed through on their way west to become missionaries to the Indians — and offered to take Janie with them —the Vedders agreed.

Janie's outraged father and uncles took after the missionaries as far as Ohio but couldn't catch up.

At Prairie du Chien, Wis., Janie and the Stevens

family caught a Mississippi River steamboat. It was taking government supplies to Ft. Snelling. Janie stayed at the fort, played with the Sioux children, moved with the Stevens family to a missionary station at Lake Harriet, and eventually wound up marrying Herman Gibbs.

*   *   *   *

Gibbs, a Vermont native, had been a teacher and a lead miner before coming to Minnesota. He and Janie built a log and sod cabin near the St. Paul-St. Anthony trail (roughly parallel to the present Larpenteur Ave. in Falcon Heights) and started farming.

Janie's Indian friends, seeing that her new husband was bald at 34, asked why "Little Crow That Was Caught" (their name for Janie) had married an "old man." They liked Gibbs, however, and named him "Prairie on Top of Head."

Prairie on Top of Head's farm prospered. A one-room frame house replaced the cabin. The one-roomer got an upstairs, four bedrooms and an "L" at the back. Four Gibbs children grew up in it.

*   *   *   *

The house still stands on its original foundations. W. Larpenteur Av. traffic rolls by its front, and Cleveland Av. traffic by its side, and it is the nucleus of the Ramsey County Historical Society's Gibbs Farm Museum.

Drive through the gate on a Sunday afternoon. There is plenty of parking space behind the broad green lawn. Twenty thousand tourists did it last summer. Children play on a playground slide, sit in an old buggy and ring the bell in the old Stoen School, a one-room type built in 1878, moved to the Gibbs Farm in 1966, and restored.

Parents and children file through the school, the house, and the society's Agricultural Museum, a red-and-white barn built to house a splendid collection of pre-gasoline, ox-powered, horse-powered and man-powered farm equipment.

* * * *

The museum is well-tended, At the door I found Susan Rood of New Brighton, dressed in a granny outfit and passing out leaflets. In an upstairs bedroom Mrs. Charlotte Pratt, society member and antique collector, was beginning another season (May 1 to Oct. 31) of quilting demonstrations with the help of another member, Mrs. John Baird, a novice.

In the kitchen Mrs. Edward J. Lettermann, co-curator with her husband, showed how to dip candles (you start dipping a string and build on that) and how to spin wool. Sunday the librarian from North Heights School, Mrs. Margaret Eubanks, would show how to churn butter.

The Lettermanns took up residence on the Gibbs Farm in 1959 in response to a help-wanted sign at the State Fair. Lettermann, at that time, was a truck paint-sprayer. He kept spraying for a few years but now has joined his wife as a full-time curator and has written a highly instructive, profusely illustrated booklet, "Farming in Minnesota," explaining early farming methods and implements.

* * * *

Upstairs in the Gibbs house there is another book for sale: *Little Bird That Was Caught* by Lillie Gibbs LeVesconte. It is the story of the "adoption," the westward journey, and the Minnesota adventures of Janie, as told to her daughter.

Lillie Gibbs LeVesconte is deceased, but she had four children. They live in Texas, Korea, Illinois and California. Five children of her brother Frank's daughter live in the Twin Cities area.

SMALL MUSEUMS

Trip No. 46 / Blanding House of Dolls

FEW OLD HOUSES enjoy a happier destiny than that of the Blanding House, snug in a hardwood forest near the end of Cemetery Road in the hills overlooking St. Croix Falls.

"Saved in the nick of time" would be an appropriate legend to be carved in old Gothic on its Italianate balustrade.

William T. Blanding, lumberman and farmer, built the house for his family of 14 about 1875. The ells on its ridge-roofed 2½-story frame spread like welcoming arms.

In its heyday friends and neighbors in formal attire ascended two flights (with continuous bannister) to the windowed attic floor, finished off for dancing.

Blanding died in 1901, and family members moved away until only two daughters, Agnes and Pearl, were left. They died in the summer of 1970 within a month of each other—Agnes at 92, Pearl at 88.

Seven years ago, Jean and Jerry Steiro, then living on Clear Lake southwest of Forest Lake, Minn., visited White Bear Lake, where Jean saw an old doll in an antique shop. She had to have it. A while later she saw another old doll at a Goodwill antique sale. Same thing.

Soon the Steiros were looking for a bigger house, one that would be appropriate for sheltering a doll museum, themselves, and their six children.

In the summer of 1970, when the Blanding sisters died, the house just stood there. The Steiros bought it and its 40 acres of woodland and moved in with their 500 dolls and six children.

The trees close over the top of Cemetery Road as you drive to the Blanding House Museum of Dolls. Just north of the house a spring sends a tiny brook into a pond by a crumbling brick "spring house," where the Blandings once made butter and hatched trout. The pond feeds a fountain in the yard.

On the other (south) side of the house we found a garden full of varicolored phlox.

Inside, the museum fills two rooms. Showcases display dolls dating from the 1840s. Jean's favorite is a French boudoir doll imported from England that has Swiss works. Wind it up, and it powders itself.

Find the house by driving up the Hwy. 8 hill through St. Croix Falls and turning left just past the Tin Man on the hilltop. Go north on the side road four-tenths of a mile and take the first road to the left. A jog in this road takes you past a hilltop cemetery where many Blandings are buried, then, through a Soo Line underpass, on Cemetery Road, to the museum.

You can also approach it from town. Turn uphill by the Ford garage on Main St. and follow State and then Vincent to Cemetery Road, the last side road to the left before reaching the Hwy. 8 underpass.

Or, coming north from Osceola, you can go through the Hwy. 8 underpass and turn right on Cemetery Road.

SMALL MUSEUMS

Trip No. 47 / Mechanical Musical Wonderland

SIXTEEN MILES BELOW the Minnesota border on Hwy. 65 at Manly, you'll see something that will stop you if you're at all alert, or at least rate a second look.

It's a kind of shopping center—on the corner of Hwys. 65 and 9—of old-fashioned stores painted in bright colors. In back there's a fenced-in compound containing a square of similarly painted buildings centered around

an imitation mountain from which gushes a waterfall.

The water plunges 40 feet into a pool, churns around, runs beneath a footbridge through a flower garden and then goes underground back to the mountain base. Irrigation pumps return it to the top through a real farm silo, which forms the mountain's hidden core.

The mountain had to be moved in piecemeal and contains, according to Tom Fretty, its owner, 5,520 tons of rock. The mountain is to amuse and entertain those who come to admire the surroundings.

The surroundings consist of a "Mechanical Music

Wonderland," with 165 major music-making mechanisms and a simulated 19th-century country town, where 72 mechanically animated life-size manikins live their programmed lives among carefully preserved relics of the past.

Among the mechanical instruments are piano, xylophone and violin nickelodeons, band organs, orchestreons, and other motorized horn, string, and percussion players, some wildly elaborate, all coordinated through perforated music rolls. All function.

They are coin-operated by the visitor, who pays an entry fee to listen and to wander along boardwalks and through museum buildings built, furnished and animated to bring back century-old village scenes such as:

- An opera house and music hall with 15 animated musicians playing taped band music. An animated magician saws a woman in half as she screams via the sound track.

- A theater showing silent films to the tune of a mechanized theater organ and piano.

- A corn cob saloon with 28 animated patrons and staff. The sound track combines saloon facts and humor with a Norwegian accent, telling how Midwest saloons were employment centers in their day, how Oly came to town and Olga shot the lights out.

- An old legal office with a full set of law books.

- An old medical office for doctor and dentist. Talking skulls do the narration.

- An old barber shop with animated shaving.

- A post office.

- A gift shop with an ice cream parlor.

- A penny arcade.

- An old-time telephone office with animated "central" and switchboard, which was brought in from Forest City, Iowa.

- A fire station with a 1856 Stein pumper, hose carts, and bell alarm.

- A general store with animated figures, cracker barrel, drugs, sundries and a photo shop.

- A little red school house, same dimensions as one Fretty attended in Faribault County, Minn.

- A blacksmith shop with buggy barn and auto barn.

- A church, built in 1932, a replica of the first Catholic church in Worthington County.

- A log cabin from Decorah, Iowa.

The piece de resistance is the mechanized music museum. Its collection includes a Paul Loche Orchestreon made in Leipzig and a Limonaire Freres machine brought to this country from France by a Limonaire foreman who came here to build hand organs and was bought out by Rudolph Wurlitzer.

Wurlitzer, whose firm later turned out the "mighty Wurlitzer" theater organs, began as a musical salesman and jobber, says Fretty, and later made it in manufacturing. Fretty has what he thinks is "the most comprehensive collection of Wurlitzer band organs in the United States—probably in the world."

Also in the museum are a Tonaphone (early nickelodeon), a Wurlitzer Kiddy band organ (smallest ever built and the only one now working of the nine that were built), a nickelodeon by the man who developed Link trainers for pilots, a Poppers (European mechanical band with ground-glass waterfall), a Locke accordian jazz player, and many more.

Fretty and his wife, Jean, grew up in Blue Earth, Minn. Fretty, after a couple of unsuccessful enterprises, opened a surplus goods store in his home in Kensett, Iowa, branched into a store uptown and expanded into more stores.

A woman asked him if he thought her farm at Hwys. 65 and 9 would make a good business location. He did, bought it and it grew into the present shopping center, "Tom's Country Market." The collector in him produced the rest of it. He had started collecting guns when he was 8, later branched into lanterns, cars and, somehow, nickel-odeons.

SMALL MUSEUMS
Trip No. 48 / Hoffman's Antique Museum

HERE THEY ARE, LIVING on Social Security in the back of a trim rectangular main street building, once their farm-equipment headquarters, then their department store, now their museum. They tenderly care for it and enjoy whatever customers appear with the price of admission. Their attractive living quarters open onto a back-yard garden.

They are Florence and Wallace Shauer. Their Hoffman Antiques Museum is not the dusty last gasp typical of some collections. It's a work of love.

It holds clocks, glass, china, pottery, kitchen, living-room and bedroom furnishings, primitive tools and implements, old general-store items, unusual costumes and jewelry, "bob wire" and other general curiosa.

One of these is a Japanese fishing float (a big glass bulb wrapped in a rope net). It broke loose and drifted across the Pacific to Port Townsend, Wash. Florence found it in a Port Townsend antique shop and couldn't resist this big, shiny, curious work of industrial art. So it hangs from the museum ceiling for all to admire.

The Shauers weren't born collectors.

Wallace, a Hoffman native, worked in the Ford plant in St. Paul and in the John Deere farm implement business, then went to Lemmon, S.D., to sell implements. There he met—"my Waterloo," he jokes.

She grew up on a ranch near Lemmon and rode horses

as a girl. Her first husband died, and she went to work for a Lemmon jeweler, learning to cut gems and make jewelry. In 1947 she married Wallace, and they ran a Bowman, N.D., furniture store for a while.

Then they returned to Wallace's home town, Hoffman (in Grant County, 23 miles west of Alexandria), where they put up a main street building for dealing in farm equipment. Times were not good. In 1952 they left their empty building and moved to Mankato. There they ran a 24-hour "truck stop" cafe on Front St. It went well.

In 1954 they returned to Hoffman to open a department store in their building. That was when the museum really began, although they didn't know it.

"I started collecting clocks," Florence said. "Then picture frames and lamps. And bowl-and-pitcher sets. Then I kind of lost control."

From there on it was everything. "Furniture—just everything."

They had their own house in Hoffman. As the collecting progressed, and Wallace caught the bug, things grew a bit cramped.

"That's why we had to move," Florence admitted. "There wasn't an inch of space any place. The house had four big walk-in closets—ideal places to store all this stuff. Then the basement got it. That held a lot. Then the garage. Finally, there was no place left.

"The best thing we could do was close out the store. It wasn't doing anything for us anyway. We closed it out and made an apartment in the back here.

"Then," she said waving around her, "we went to work."

She stepped around behind one of the admirable results, a shiny glass counter full of fine glass items. On a high shelf behind her ranged 30 mantel clocks.

We were off on the tour. Florence supplied most of the running commentary. Wallace filled in.

"We did most of our collecting around here," Florence said. "We didn't travel a lot. Brought a van-load home from Washington and Montana one year . . . .

"These plates, from Bozeman, were made in England for first members of the Stockmen's Association—Wedgewood . . . .

"These vases are called Croesus glass. They come in purple, clear and green . . . .

"This is Spode [china produced in Staffordshire, England] . . . .

"These are Bavarian and Prussian cracker jars . . . ."

There were room assemblies. A kitchen showing 20 years of collecting. There was a china closet whose beautiful carving had been covered by paint.

"We hauled it to Fargo and had it dipped in acid," Florence said.

There was a high chair, similarly carved. Its craftsman had joined and assembled it for readjustment into a go-cart.

The Shauers had stored an antique kitchen stove in their garage. "Chickens roosted in it," Wallace said. "Brought it out here in the country. Beautiful after we got all the dirt off."

A living room display boasted a "Faultless" wood stove, American made, extremely ornate. Here, too, was a soapstone tobacco humidor whose fantastic oily-looking animals were carved under water by the Chinese.

Down the line, an elaborate hall tree, two mirrors, coat hangers, and a grandfather clock with a big pendulum "came from the old Shurnuff Co. in Minneapolis . . . ."

And so it went, much too much to take in at one time. Old love seat with two chairs. Old horn phonograph.

Queen Anne chair. Spinning wheel (worn foot pedal shows much use). Costume jewelry and fans. Little agate cowboy boots, cut, polished and made into earrings by Florence when she was working for the Lemmon jeweler.

Magnificent carved-wood double bed with hand-made quilt. "Company sleeps here," Florence said.

Old schoolhouse water cooler, apple peelers, egg beaters, snuff jars.

Fine old book sets (Macaulay's *Essays, Masterpieces and the History of Literature* edited by Julian Hawthorne, John Russell Young, John Porter Lamberton and Oliver H. G. Leigh, with 40 photogravure plates, in 10 volumes —Greek, Latin, Persian, Arabian, Italian, Spanish, French, Scandinavian, German classics.

Stone Mason fruit jars, pure rye whiskey jug, Red Wing Union Stoneware, Union Leader Cut Plug container, Horse Shoe snuff, portable post office (boxes, window, letter slot) from Effington, S.D., old shaving horse (put your foot there, step on this thing and pull a draw-knife).

If you can't take it all in, you can always return. Give the Shauers a ring in advance, and they'll be ready for you.

SMALL MUSEUMS
Trip No. 49 / Carver County

THE CARVER COUNTY Historical Society has a model museum. It's in Waconia, 30 miles southeast of Minneapolis on Hwy. 5.

It is neat, well-organized, well-attended, well cared

for and informative, and upon seeing it one can only say, "Every county should have one."

You can see it any Sunday, Tuesday or Friday from 1 p.m., autumn, winter, spring or summer, and when you do, one of the 10 directors will be on hand to answer your questions.

They are on a rotating schedule. Beside that, if you happen to be in town during the off-hours and want somebody to show you through, you can telephone

Joseph Braunworth or Reuben Aretz. They are "on call."

What prompts such devotion to duty on the part of the directors? They're retired. They welcome this special interest. Braunworth was the Ford dealer in Waconia for 27 years.

The museum organization's hero, who died before his dream reached fruition, was O. D. Sell, retired general store owner. Sell founded the Carver County Historical Society and was its president from 1940 to 1960.

In the late 1950s the County Board made the crucial decision to provide funds. It nearly decided, also, to build the museum in Chaska, the county seat.

"They decided that wouldn't be fair," Braunworth recalls, "because the Waconia people had worked for the museum."

It had been housed in crowded Waconia quarters in the school and then the city hall over the years. O. D. Sell died shortly before the new building was done. "We felt very bad about that," says Braunworth.

A picture of Sell, in a handsome antique frame, hangs just to the left of the stairway facing you as you enter.

The museum houses antiques from homes throughout the county, dating to its beginning, and some Indian artifacts and buffalo skulls dating before that.

It is especially strong for its ancient typewriter collection and well over 100 hunting and fowling pieces, including a four-barrel combination vari-calibered, vari-gauged rifle and shotgun, a monster to lift.

There are catalogued shelves of old books, many in Swedish and German, a well-kept file of old photographs and hard-cover files of newspapers from around the county. County residents browse through them for Grandpa's auction notice and other memorabilia.

The society has received so many gifts of family portraits from generations past that it has to keep most of them in a store room and rotate the displays. The hosts then have to mollify families who happen in when their particular contributions are resting in the back stretch.

Dandy tour: After looking at the flood photographs in the Carver County Museum take Carver County Road 10 from Waconia to Chaska and look at the elevation work on the dirt dike along the Minnesota River.

SMALL MUSEUMS

Trip No. 50 / Hennepin County

Do you like to bring your friends up short with "Did you know that . . ." questions like, "Did you know that Hennepin County came within three votes of being named 'Snelling County' in 1851?"

Or: "Did you know that hens once were so scarce in Hennepin County that each egg was weighed individually?"

Or: "Did you know that Hennepin County farmers made wooden shoes to save their leather ones for good?"

Or: "Did you know that many early settlers had to walk from what is now Wayzata to what is now Minneapolis with sacks of flour on their backs?"

Such ploys are easy after a visit to the Hennepin County Historical Society Museum at 2303 3rd Av. S., a block north of the Minneapolis Institute of Arts.

This museum, little-known to many, is two things: (1) a filed repository of historical detail (photographic, printed, handwritten) about Hennepin County and (2) a far-out collection of curiosa and memorabilia which brings back the flavor and temper of an earlier day as little else can. Movies, dramatic art, painting, sculpture, music and literature can do it, but not the way an egg-scale can.

Children know the museum's benefits more than adults, at least now that the kids are being brought in by the school-bus load. I attached myself to a group from Savage, Minn., 22 second and third-graders with their teacher, Mary Senne.

"They don't act like savages," joked museum director Joe Justad.

"They can," Miss Senne assured him.

They were a lively, inquisitive group and seemed to enjoy the visit under the firm hand of their Junior League guide, Mrs. Robert McCrea. The Junior Leaguers see it as their civic duty to provide the museum with competent guides four or five days a week.

They study for it, and a good thing, too. The kids know all the questions, about as many as there are items in the museum. Nobody could know all the answers, but Mrs. McCrea knew more than I.

She handled the kids with the confidence of a coast artillery top-kick. "Please don't ask questions until I've finished," she ordered as the kids waved their hands in the middle of her commentary. It was a good one. For example, in the blacksmith shop room: "The blacksmith was an important man in his community. (Please don't sit on the bellows, boys.) He not only shoed the horses, but he made the tools." And so on.

Later she had some fun holding up a horsetail flybrush and asking the kids what they thought it was for. They missed that one but guessed the egg-scale.

148

I was surprised to learn that Lincoln's funeral car burned years after the assassination, when it was a traveling exhibit. The museum has its brake lever, alongside a *Minneapolis Journal* account headed, "Car That Carried Remains of Lincoln Burned in Spectacular Prairie Fire."

This and the Civil War saddle, uniforms, drum and other relics seemed to interest the kids less than the old-fashioned school-room where they sat in the desks, slyly tried on the dunce cap, and curiously put their fingers in the ink-well holes.

The big hit was "Main Street, U.S.A.," an incredibly detailed miniature reproduction of 11 buildings, 30 years in the making, created by Edna Knowles King.

CHAPTER VIII SOUTHERN AND WESTERN PLAINS

Trip No. 51 / Pipestone

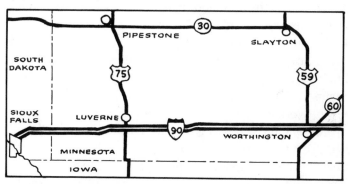

"The site of the quarries was a sacred place, known to the tribesmen of a large part of the continent . . . it is not too much to say that the great Pipestone Quarry was the most important single locality in aboriginal geography and lore." —John Wesley Powell, director of the Bureau of Ethnology, Smithsonian Institution, 1879-1902.

THE FOREGOING REMARKS are framed in the attractive air-conditioned automated museum and headquarters building in the Pipestone National Monument grounds on the northwest edge of Pipestone, Minn.

151

"We want people to see it," my guide told me. "There is some disagreement among scholars. We're proud of this quotation."

There can be no disagreement about the high level of the Pipestoners' pride.

My guide was a teacher of industrial arts in the Pipestone High School.

"My Minneapolis friends ask me why I want to stay out here in Pipestone," said he. "Well, we love it here. You should see it in the spring when the prairie flowers are blooming."

Beyond that, he pointed out, Pipestone has a dandy school system and takes a big interest in its young people. This is evident in its school bands, its YMCA, its Little League, its parks and its swimming and wading pools which employ six lifeguards.

He showed me into a small theater and pushed a button. Color slides and a recorded voice explained how Indians split the hard quartzite to get down several feet to the workable red clay-like catlanite or pipestone. Legend tells them this was blood of their ancestors who were drowned in the big flood.

Next, with guidebooks in hand, I took a well-marked hour's walk along "Circle Trail." Then Indians burned off prairies so often, to kill the mosquitoes, that there weren't any trees around here in the old days, but trees have grown up. You go through the woods across Pipestone Creek, by active quarries, past where the creek falls over a quartzite ledge. The walk abounds in legend, explained in a guidebook.

At the quarry I found Harvey Derby ("Running Elk"), his wares spread under a canopy. He had the regular carpenter's saw and implements used to work the pipestone into souvenirs. He told me his grandfather,

152

from Sisseton, S. D., made pipes in the same place.

Across the road from the monument grounds, around a pool deep enough so that one can dive off its banks into eight feet of water, you will see the outdoor theater for Pipestone's Hiawatha Pageant.

Over the last 14 years the pageant has become an ever-growing and absorbing civic interest among dyed-in-the-wool Pipestoners and a major factor, along with the ancient quarry grounds, in attracting tourists to the area.

The Hiawatha Pageant Club, made up of local businessmen, has put something like $100,000 into buying and developing the grounds, buildings and equipment.

SOUTHERN AND WESTERN PLAINS
Trip No. 52 / Madelia

I DARESAY I HAD the world's best guide for a nostalgic-historical 30-mile circle tour west and northwest of Madelia, Minn., through LaSalle and Hanska.

His name was Albert Shelley.

He grew up in the country west of Madelia, and he farmed there. His boyhood swimming hole was on the southeast shore of Lake Hanska, which is 9 miles long and 8 miles northwest of town.

Shelley's name once was "Sjelle" (Norwegian). He was born in Watonwan County. His mother told him of the excitement that swept the countryside when the Younger boys, part of the Jesse James gang, were surrounded, one of them killed and the rest captured beside the Watonwan

153

River (North Fork) straight south of LaSalle. That was in 1876.

Shelley had much pride in the land. It was rich in memories for him. He enjoyed showing me around the old nostalgic places.

We drove a mile north of Madelia on state Hwy. 15, then 8 miles west on the LaSalle Road along the Watonwan River. Even with LaSalle, we jogged left to look at a monument:

"Younger brothers captured at this location Sept. 21, 1876 . . ."

From here we headed north through LaSalle for 4 miles to Watonwan County Road 6, turned right a short way and then left (north again) on Brown County Road 11. Less than a mile on this road brought us to a smoothly rounded grassy hill on our right, topped by some bushy, thrifty-looking cedars.

Turning up a well-packed dirt trail, we drove near the top and got out on the fine, smoothly bent grass. There we had a long view of part of Lake Hanska. We were on Indian Hill.

Said Shelley: "This is Indian burial ground. The biologists are interested in this hill. It's virgin soil. It has never been turned by a plow."

I looked down and found lavender crocuses anchored to their short furry stems and ruffling in the wind with the grasstops.

We looked across at Lake Hanska (from "hanske," Norwegian for glove). Shelley said his old swimming hole was near the point. "This was a hunters' paradise—duck, prairie chickens."

Heading north, we saw ducks. In about a mile we came to a "Fort Hill" sign. A few rods beyond the fence on the left once stood a fort where troops were stationed to protect settlers from Indians in 1862. Later the pretty woods around the fort, sloping down to the lake, became a picnic ground.

"There was a flagpole you could see for miles," said Shelley. "When the flag was flying, the picnic was on. The woods would be full of carriages."

Heading back east to Hwy. 15 we went through Hanska where, said Shelley, "every Fourth of July there is a celebration in the park."

On our left, as we passed Linden Lake, we saw a monument to John Armstrong, early county supervisor, who was killed by Sioux on the lakeshore in 1862.

Shelley and I parted at his neat house where he did his own housekeeping.

On the way home I thought of the train depot. In Shelley's boyhood it had been the center of excitement. Now, he said, "It's the loneliest place in town."

Madelia has since developed an excellent historical museum.

SOUTHERN AND WESTERN PLAINS
Trip No. 53 / Albert Lea and Austin

EARLY SPRING IS a good time to roll southward for a look at two of our more interesting population centers near the Iowa border — Albert Lea and Austin, Minn.

Growing things are a little further advanced down there at this time of year. The rich fields are turning green, and the countryside has a pleasant look.

There is quite a bit of four-lane divided highway on either of two routes from the Twin Cities.

Hwy. 65 and its super-ego, Interstate 35, are the most direct way to Albert Lea, of course.

Returning from Austin (18 miles east of Albert Lea), if you're looking for a different route, divided highways all the way to Cannon Falls, via Rochester, won't make it seem too far out of the way.

A casual drive around Austin and Albert Lea may come as something of a surprise if you're a stranger to that section and think of it simply as farming country. These are well-developed communities with substantial civic assets.

Explorer Joseph N. Nicollet named Albert Lea after Col. Albert M. Lea of the U. S. Dragoons (a term no longer used in the army but which then referred to troops trained to serve either on foot or horseback).

Lea surveyed the area in 1835, and the city was founded 23 years later. The story goes that a horse race (Old Tom vs. Itasca Fly) with heavy bets of cash and real estate riding on it decided whether Albert Lea or a nearby town-site called Itasca would be the Freeborn County seat. Old Tom won, and today there's no more Itasca in that part of the state.

There is plenty of Albert Lea, however. Its most charming and prepossessing asset is Fountain Lake.

The business section with its big water tower touches on one shore. The rest is handsome residential area, bathing beach, picnic grounds, a small island with a bridge to it, a roadside park with tables, and a dignified looking Albert Lea Country Club (golf, pool, white frame clubhouse), of many years' standing.

Near the north side of the lake the Northeast Junior High School occupies an interesting fortress-like cir-

cular building. South of town spreads an ambitiously
planned industrial park, which the Chamber of Commerce is plugging.

Joined to Fountain Lake and spreading over many
times its area to the southeast and east lies Albert Lea
Lake. Hwy. 38, running south from the Austin road
(Hwy.16) will take you to Helmer Myre State Park (camping, picnics, boat landing and big deciduous trees) on Albert Lea Lake's irregular shore.

Going east, Hwy. 16 will take you into Interstate 90 to Austin, seat of Mower County and home of the Geo. A. Hormel Packing Co. It was founded in 1856 and named for its first settler, Austin R. Nicholas.

While Austin doesn't have Albert Lea's water acreage, it has the Red Cedar River (dredged and beautified in 1963-64) running through it, Dobbins Creek, which widens into small East Side Lake before joining the river near the center of town, and Turtle Creek coming in from the west.

Turtle Creek and 8th Av. NW. run under Interstate 90 just south of a broad triangle near the northwest corner of town where Austin Junior College stands.

Driving east on 8th Av. NW. will take you to a "T" where, by taking four southeasterly jogs you can cross Main St. into 4th St. NE. back to Interstate 90. By driving under the throughway and turning first right, then left on 8th St. NE. you will be on your way to Todd Park, a big one with many picnic tables (opening date, May 1).

In the course of getting from 8th Av. NW. to Main St. you will pass the YMCA Community Center. On the way from there to Todd Park, you'll pass a Hormel-endowed University of Minnesota research center.

Back on Interstate 90 going east, you're on your way to Rochester.

158

SOUTHERN AND WESTERN PLAINS

Trip No. 54 / Hormel Nature Center

DRIVING THROUGH Austin on east-west bound I-90, you'll find an interesting nature center just north of it, by taking the 21st St. exit.

Just north and east of the exit a very thick stand of spruce and other evergreens muffles the noises from the freeway and serves as a winter hang-out for wild deer in the area. The trees were planted by Jay C. Hormel.

His father, George A. Hormel, started the Hormel packing plant, Austin's big industry. George A. died in 1946, Jay C. in 1954, having put the packing firm in the hands of a group of trusted Austin men.

The family moved west. Only George A. (Geordie) Hormel II, jazz pianist and entrepreneur, returned to run the old family mansion as Kings Wood Hotel in the 1960s, then sold it to the Oblate Fathers, who are selling it to a private concern to use as a treatment center for emotionally disturbed pre-adolescents.

That includes the core area containing the buildings (gatehouse, stables, auxiliary buildings and 97-room mansion) but not the rest, 123 acres of savannalike grassland, tall timber, a pond and two branches of spring-fed Dobbin's Creek. These acres are the Jay C. Hormel Nature Center.

In 1970 the federal and state governments (Land and Water Conservation Fund) bought the Center land for

159

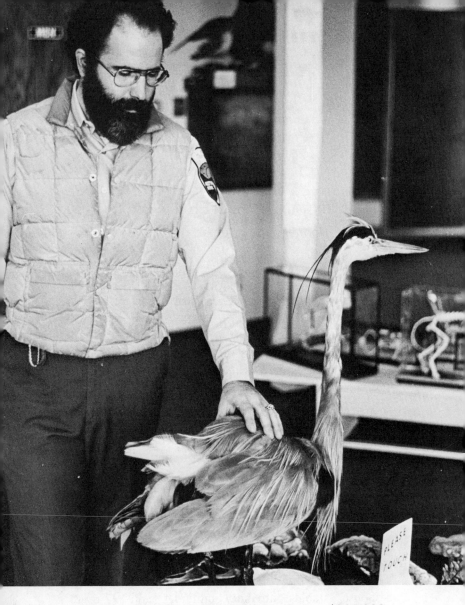

the city of Austin to administrate. Price, $230,000.

In 1971, the state and the Hormel Foundation paid $14,000 each and the federal government $28,000 for improvements—parking lot, pond, several bridges, 2.5 miles of pedestrian trails—strechable to three miles of cross-country ski trails.

In 1974 the Ober Foundation of St. Paul (founded by Agnes Ober with assets of $12.5 million for education, health conservation, social services, senior citizens, the arts) put up $57,500 toward an interpretive building and program.

Richard Birger, formerly of Woodlake Nature Center, Richfield, before that a cattle buyer and animal husbandry graduate, was hired as director.

A ground-hugging interpretive building, with an exposed basement floor overlooking the woods and with the upper floor on parking lot level, commands views of woods and grassland where prairie grasses are being nurtured. It was built by volunteers. That is, construction work was done by the Austin Area Vocational-Technical Institute carpentry class, wiring by the institute's electrical class, and sheet metal and plumbing by area apprenticeship classes.

Outside you can find a beaver dam, woodpecker holes, grasses, and a barred owl's retreat inside a tall elm that is bare of bark—dead so long nobody knew at the time what was killing it. You may also see, at times, stray unfenced deer who wander in for browsing and shelter.

Inside are live snakes, opossums, fish, stuffed birds and animals, and human and animal skeletons. "Touch and see." Kneel and peer through a hole near the floor to see a fox snake named "Shadrack." Meet him on his own terms.

Outside, you can wander around the trails—or ski, snow permitting—to view the trees. Jay C. Hormel had tried to grow every species in North America on these grounds. Many died. During a period of neglect the labels of some were vandalized. Tree identification is difficult. However, Jay Hormel's arboretum records exist. In time, order may be restored.

SOUTHERN AND WESTERN PLAINS

Trip No. 55 / Mountain Lake

A LAKE THAT ONCE existed a few miles east of town was drained during the march of agriculture; soybeans grow there now. A hill or "mountain" in the middle of the lake (vertical rise about 50 feet) was an ancient Indian campsite. Now it's a county park.

So it is that the name Mountain Lake is locked into the past. You'll learn this and a good deal more about Mountain Lake's heritage if you're lucky enough to talk with Henry Kliewer, president of Heritage House, Inc., a nonprofit group dedicated to preserving nostalgic memorabilia.

The group only recently has leaped forward by setting up a Heritage House Village on part of 22 acres it has acquired just beyond the town's east edge. The village has an old farmhouse with attached barn, a chapel, a general store, a country schoolhouse, a blacksmith shop, a depot with freight department and a caboose on a section of real track.

Kliewer and his wife, Sue, are Mennonites. They have the best family picture I ever saw. It was taken with help from a maple tree last Easter before the leaves came out. Children and grandchildren are sitting in the branches; parents and grandparents are standing underneath.

Many Mennonites came to this country from southern Russia, where they had moved from Holland, Germany,

162

Austria and other countries because of their conscientious objection to military service. When Russia made service mandatory, they came here. Mountain Lake has a big Mennonite church.

The Mennonites spoke German in their various countries of residence. They organized in Zurich, Switzerland, in 1525 and took their name from Menno Simons, who was their leader in Holland. Stress was laid on discipline rather than dogma.

Henry Kliewer served 43 years for the North Star Telephone Co. and was plant superintendent in five counties (Cottonwood, Watonwan, Jackson, Martin and Brown) when he retired a few years back. Sue was the Mountain Lake librarian. They have a son, a daughter and grandchildren.

In retirement Henry threw himself into the Heritage project with the zest of a born collector. (He has a fine collection of vintage telephones.)

Heritage House, Inc., which he heads, has 135 voting

members at a C-note each and during the Bicentennial got $3,000 from the State Historical Society. "Helped tremendously," Henry said.

He accompanied my wife and me to Heritage House Village and gave us a guided tour. First he showed us the chapel. It had been a hired man's house, now remodeled into a chapel and furnished with religious artifacts. It has a steeple, authentic pews, and stained-glass windows. Services involving small groups—and board meetings— have been held here. It's heatable in winter. The chapel organ, built in 1898, came from a collection of three stored in a local shed for 19 years. Henry cleaned and restored it "piece by piece."

The farmhouse and adjoining barn, vintage 1884, both excellent museum pieces, were moved in from the country. In the house an old chest is carved in Germanic style with the owner's American destination. A similar chest cover, made into a coffee table, can be seen in Henry's living room.

Original occupants of the village farmhouse came from Pordenau, south Russia. Many have contributed to its furnishing. Fashionable clothes hang on hooks carved of wood. Antique photos help bring some of it back to life. In the kitchen you'll find a brick oven that restorers built using old iron fixtures. There's a rock-laden rotating mangle that calls for real muscle.

The barn has a logging sled and a hand-crank corn sheller. The general store, moved in from Darfur, 14 miles northeast, contains pipes, jugs, chewing tobacco, embroidery silk, patent medicines, an old counter paper roller, a ceiling suspension for wrapping string, a ribbon cabinet, celluloid collars, and an insulated Smith Sanitary Bubbler drinking fountain. Too much more even to list.

The schoolhouse has a fine collection of antique graduating-class photos, old scrapbooks and shelves of old schoolbooks.

The depot, bought from Burlington Northern for $1, holds a variety of artifacts yet to be sorted out. Among them are a primitive x-ray machine, an old hand loom, a dandy hall tree and land documents signed by Teddy Roosevelt and Woodrow Wilson.

Toward the tour's end we met two young Mennonite women, Marijke Paternotte and Ria Belier, both here from Holland on an exchange program. Phyllis Ratzlaff, living in the area and working on the project, was showing them around.

Before leaving, we got directions to Mountain Park, where the lake once existed, south of the Hwy. 60 grain elevator east of town. The park occupies the erstwhile mountain island, now nicely wooded in a sea of soybeans.

Off the Mountain Lake Range, a collection of old recipes and customs brought over by early settlers, covers hard-to-pronounce goodies, holiday observances, and the way many things were done. It is available from Heritage House, Box 386, Mountain Lake, Minn. 56159.

CHAPTER IX FESTIVALS

Trip No. 56 / Kenyon

JOE GATES, MY OLD SCHOOLMATE, was the pledgemaster in our fraternity house at the University of Minnesota. He ruled the freshmen with a paddle.

"What is the garden spot of North America?" he would ask. The only acceptable answer was "Kenyon, Minnesota." Kenyon was Joe's home town. You reach it by driving south from the Twin Cities on Hwys. 52 and 56.

*   *   *

Kenyon is a modest town on the upper Zumbro River, where the Zumbro is only a creek. The creek forms a green little valley of leafy trees and thick grass where a few horses graze.

Kenyon has a well-patronized municipal swimming pool (built in 1956) with a separate wading pool for the youngsters, an excellent facility for a town of 1,624. Its special pride is of more recent origin — a "Boulevard of Roses."

*   *   *

Several years ago, Lloyd Jystad, who takes care of the Kenyon swimming pool and keeps the waste treatment plant perking along, suggested planting some roses in the center boulevard which divides the west end of the main street along Hwy. 60. The suggestion led to the fanciest blooming of tree roses along any street I know. Joe Gates would be flabbergasted.

Such things don't come easily. Before the big blooming came a barrage of fund drives, pep talks and general
badgering by a hard core of Kenyon rose-fanciers pres-
ently headed by Harold Severson, president of the Kenyon Boulevard of Roses Society. Jystad is vice-president,
Earl Fredrickson secretary-treasurer and Clarence O.
Jensen director. Fredrickson works for Kenyon Municipal Utilities and Jensen owns an auto repair shop.

*   *   *

I never heard of a civic project that didn't encounter
resistance. Roses are no exception. Said Severson: "We
have a councilman who would like to 'plow the roses
under.' "

You can see that the rose boosters had to push pretty
hard.

*   *   *

Frank Callister, editor and publisher of the *Kenyon
Leader,* has been the very model of cooperation. He runs
names of rose project donors right down to the $1 variety,
in the *Leader*. In 1967, the first year in which the Rose
boosters elected to put on a pageant and pick a Rose
Queen, the *Leader* reported:

"Lady Bird Endorses Boulevard of Roses Project."

The first Rose Queen was LaDonna Aaker, 17.

The Boulevard of Roses has four blocks of "tree roses."
They take a lot of special treatment, including fall burial
and spring resurrection. Some bear three varieties on a
single stem. New lights illuminate them.

Said Severson, "Rosarians say this may be the only
community planting of tree roses in the Midwest, possi-
bly in the entire nation."

FESTIVALS
Trip No. 57 / Faribault

AROUND JUNE 20 IS THE time to drive down Interstate Hwy. 35 to Faribault, Minn., for its Western Roundup Days weekend festival.

The new name was picked because the Cannon Valley Saddle Club's horse show has been such a hit each year in Faribault that the festival leaders decided to go all the way.

The western parade usually starts at 2 p.m., Saturday. It may include sheriffs' "posses" from different counties. Starting at 8 a.m. Sunday at the Rice County Fairgrounds, the horse show is on all day with just about every kind of riding and judging of horsemanship—bareback riding, egg and spoon carrying, polo weaving and all the rest.

Other things will be going on, not all "western." The Faribault Art Center has its annual art show, and girls compete for the regional dairy princess title.

*   *   *

Of course, a major attraction for years has been the annual peony show at the Brand Peony Farm on the southeast edge of Faribault, a block south of Hwy. 60. (See Trip 66.)

Another big attraction is the town itself. Drive through the business section and it looks like any town, but you can find some remarkable views.

For example, look down the Straight River from the

169

3rd St. bridge, glimpse the town from the high bank by St. Mary's Hall, Episcopal boarding school for girls, or stand by the woolen mill on Hwy. 3 on the north side of town where the Cannon River goes over a dam and look across.

The dam runs into a little point where, if there isn't a car already parked there, you can eat lunch.

At the Brand Peony Farm you'll see some of the world's finest peony plants.

There was a regular traffic jam at the farm a week ago. People of all ages were looking at the flowers, and nearly everyone I talked to had been there before.

*   *   *

You can arrange for a guided tour through the Treasure Cave Cheese Co. caves in the sandstone bank of the Straight River at 3rd St. on any day except Sunday.

*   *   *

Interstate Hwy. 35 has made the 50-mile drive south from the Twin Cities to Faribault an easy one, little more

than a hop and a skip. It's throughway most of the way.

There is a lot of recreation in the surrounding country. West of town you have better than a dozen sandy lakes good for fishing, swimming, sailing and water skiing if you pick the right ones and the right weather. The Straight River runs north through town. It joins the Cannon near the woolen mill.

Kids swim and fish in the pond below the falls in summer. From here the Cannon wanders northeast through Nerstrand Woods State Park, which can be reached by Rice County Road 20 going east out of town.

You follow 20 to Cannon Falls, to Nerstrand, and 40 (a gravel road) to the park. It's mainly for hiking and camping — 4,000 acres, picnic grounds, trailer and campsites, running water. The trees are hardwood, and there is a small waterfall. It's 10 miles from Faribault.

For just a short sightseeing jaunt, though, you'll want to drive around on the high side of the Straight River for a look at Shattuck School (fine stonework, handsome chapel), St. Mary's, and the Minnesota School for the Deaf.

FESTIVALS

Trip No. 58 / Waterville

"WHEN YOU GET UP as far north as the Twin Cities," said Walter Merten, "they don't eat bullheads."

Some do, of course, but Merten had a point. He should. He's in the bullhead business. He runs a fish market on the northwest shore of Lake Sakatah in Waterville, Minn., 60 miles south of Minneapolis. Waterville calls itself "The Bullhead Capital of the World."

Last year during "Bullhead Day," an annual Waterville festival, Mr. and Mrs. Merten and Merten's mother, Martha, "pan dressed" around 13,000 bullheads.

Pan dress means they cut off the head, skin the fish, take out its insides, cut off its fins and wash it so it's ready to fry. The charge for this service is 3 cents a fish.

It doesn't really bother Walter that he doesn't get many customers from the Twin Cities. If he did, he probably wouldn't know what to do. As it is, he gets so many from other places that he doesn't know what to do.

"We had to get rid of our telephone," Mrs. Merten said. "They'd call us up at three in the morning to ask us how the fishing was."

Where do all the customers come from? From the south.

According to Jim Rohl, town barber, it took Iowans to wake up the Waterville natives to nature's bounty.

Admittedly, the bullhead is not a handsome fish by Arrow Collar standards.

Don't let its whiskers fool you.

Writes Roger Preuss, wildlife artist and Waterville native son, on one of his wildlife calendars:

"It is quite a sight to see whole families of bullhead fishermen converge on Waterville . . . license plates from Iowa, and Illinois, from Indiana and Nebraska . . . It seems difficult for many observers to understand . . .

*   *   *

"Well, if you know . . . the aroma and supreme flavor of a mess of fresh-caught pan-fried bullheads, you have the answer . . ."

*   *   *

Preuss was a leader in starting Bullhead Days and also "Waterville Bullhead Time," which he explains this way:

"With clocks set one half hour ahead of world time . . . you can catch your limit in 30 minutes and be on your way again without having lost any time."

*   *   *

If you like to pack a picnic lunch, this trip will give you a chance to eat it in one of Minnesota's newest state parks.

The Cannon River widens into a number of lakes as it passes through Waterville and to the west and east of it. One of these, starting in Waterville and stretching eastward, is Upper Sakatah Lake. Along its south shore stretches 850-acre Sakatah State Park.

The park entrance is on Hwy. 60 as you approach Waterville from the east.

*   *   *

Here are some of the lakes around Waterville where natives say the bullhead fishing is especially good (in addition to heavily fished Lake Sakatah and Lower Sakatah):

Elysian, Reeds, Sprague, Horse Shoe, Sunfish, Sabre, Sasse, Charles, and Jefferson. Lake Francis, according to Allan D. Willcox, editor and publisher of the *Waterville Advance,* has a special breed, very large and tasty.

FESTIVALS
Trip No. 59 / New London

TWO TRAPPERS BUILT a dam on the middle fork of the upper Crow River in 1878, and today there's a town there—New London, Minn.

The dam has been rebuilt and now the millpond above it makes New London one of the most attractive towns of its size (population 721) in the Upper Midwest.

The millpond connects with several miles of winding, island-dotted navigable watercourse. This makes New London a water recreation center and the millpond a setting for a summer water show.

In the summer, usually in mid-July, New London puts on something called Water Show and Fun Days. It includes horseshoe pitching, track events for the children, barbershop singing, watermelon by the millpond, speedboat races, a Crow River canoe derby, water skiing, a water show, and fireworks.

New Londoners take pride in their speedy fireworks shooting. They like to see them go up in a blaze of glory.

The water show on the millpond is usually a crazy, pick-up kind of affair. One year a "banana boat" showed up from Spicer. It had a tower in the middle with a swivel hitch for a water skier. Somehow it got the skier making circles in one direction and itself making smaller circles in the opposite drecton — a big hit. The performers worked for no pay. In fact, they weren't even expected.

175

On another occasion some New Londoners rigged up two pontoon boats to look like the *Monitor* and the *Merrimac* and blasted away at each other through stove-pipes disguised as cannons until the *Monitor* sheared a pin and drifted ashore by the lumberyard.

On quieter weekends New London can be fun for its National Fish Hatchery, which can put out four million walleyes, a million bass and a million and a half bluegills in a season without batting an eye, and for the hatchery's classy little aquarium with air conditioning. Its tanks display:

Walleye, sucker, northern pike, sauger, black crappie, bluegill, rainbow trout, brown trout, lake trout, brook trout, largemouth and smallmouth bass, dogfish, carp, sheepshead, lake sturgeon, black bullhead, shortnose and longnose gar and American eel.

The hatchery has 16 rearing ponds covering 46 acres along the Crow. In a sense, you might say that the fish that come out of them to stock lakes across the Upper Midwest are fed hay. In a manner of speaking.

High grade alfalfa hay goes into the pond (this is called "fertilizing"). Bacteria go to work, and the hay becomes food for plankton (floating or weakly swimming plant and animal life such as water fleas, copepods, diatoms and midges). The young fish eat the plankton.

Right behind the aquarium in town the Crow runs out of a pretty lake through a dam below which many panfish gather on the hatchery grounds. Here people under 16 are allowed to fish.

To reach New London go northwest on Hwy. 55 (Olson Memorial Drive) to Paynesville. Turn south there on Hwy. 23.

Don't miss the National Fish Hatchery aquarium right by the New London millpond dam.

CHAPTER X   CAMPS

Trip No. 60 / El Rancho Manana

"KOOP'S ACRES," it used to be called.

Now it's "El Rancho Manana," campers' ranch.

*   *   *   *

About twenty years ago Dr. Herman Koop, Cold Spring, Minn., general practitioner, decided he wanted to keep a few horses and do some riding. He bought a strip of land for the horses 7½ miles northwest of Cold Spring, which is 20 miles southwest of St. Cloud on Hwy. 23.

He bought in a hilly, picturesque, mostly wooded area dotted with sandy lakes and ponds. The first piece included a sandy swimming beach on Long Lake. As more land became available, he started buying along a creek coming down from the north.

After following the creek for about 1¼ mile, he took a right angle and started buying land in an easterly direction. He wound up with a big inverted "L" covering 1,208 acres. "Koop's Acres."

*   *   *

As the years went by, Koop had a bulldozer build a series of dikes across the creek to make more wetlands for the waterfowl. Then he started incubating mallards and releasing them along the creek, feeding them and inviting friends in for the fall hunting.

A few years ago the Conservation Department evinced an interest in this operation, and the doctor stopped it because of rules and regulations.

There the land sat until 1964. Son-in-law Dick Ward, husband of Koop's daughter "Toy" (Rosemary), Dick's brother Louis and his wife, Betty, then got the El Rancho Manana idea.

It took them a while to talk the doctor into letting them go ahead, with an option to buy, but he finally did.

They went ahead with energy, and the campers responded with enthusiasm.

They started coming in on opening day, Aug. 1, 1964, and helped the Wards nail together the first privies. The customers kept coming through fall, and winter didn't stop them.

"The joint was jumping on winter weekends," Louis recalls. "We really didn't expect it."

The entrepreneurs hastily bought some oil heaters for the uninsulated headquarters building. With the heaters going, the inside thermometers held steady at 50° F. Outside everyone rode snowmobiles.

During the heavy snows of late winter a contingent of the National Guard helped rescue the horses.

The Wards employ college and high school students as trail guides, campground keepers, bathhouse cleaners, hay makers and garbage haulers.

There *are* a few frills: a donkey cart shuttle between headquarters and the campgrounds. Odd shapes of plywood hang around in the woods. Whoever brings one in gets a prize.

The ranch has a hill called "Old Smoky." It commands a view and might become a skiing site. There are hiking trails, rental boats, deer, wild berries, hazel nuts, and play areas.

CAMPS

Trip No. 61 / Camp on the Mississippi

ONE OF THE MOST flourishing of the growing number of camp grounds privately owned and operated in Minnesota is a place called "Camp, on the Mississippi" 4 miles upstream from Elk River.

You find it by driving 3 miles northeast toward St. Cloud on Hwy. 10, measuring from the mid-town stop light in Elk River and then turning south to the river's north bank. Or you can just stick as close as possible to the river as you drive northeast out of town.

The owners thought it prudent to invest $25,000 in a 20-by-50-by-30-foot swimming pool (fanning out at the shallow end) with heated, filtered, circulating water, plus a separate wading pool.

The camp's 60 acres along the river, about 20 feet above the water level, have an open, airy look, in the shady groves along the shore and the grassy fields behind. There are different levels and foliated divisions which give campers a degree of privacy. There also is space for group fun and team sports. You can rent tents, tent-trailers, stoves, lanterns, canoes, boats and saddle horses.

"Boat floats" and hayrides are available for a fee.

On a boat float you get driven upstream 12 or 18 miles (your choice) in a group, put in a canoe or rowboat, as you prefer, and let it float back to camp. The shorter ride takes about four hours, the longer most of the day—very popular.

Most campers seem to be extroverts. They enjoy group activities and having people around, but not always. One couple spent a honeymoon here. The groom reserved a secluded spot a week in advance and the pair arrived after dark. In the morning they woke up to a "charivari."

Finally, there's the management—a United Air Lines pilot, his wife, and their eight children.

The Hellerstedts bought the land, once a truck farm, in December 1962 and began, right in the middle of the winter, to start clearing out the brush along the river.

Winter was a good time for it—no leaves to obscure vision and no bugs. Since then the family has been equally busy with campers, rental equipment and horses on which some of the older children now serve as trail guides.

"When we lived in the city," recalled Bill Hellerstedt's wife Geri, "the children got bored and asked, 'What can we do?' They never ask any more."

CAMPS
Trip No. 62 / Interstate Park

THE DEMAND FOR summertime camping space usually fills Interstate Park on the St. Croix River at Taylor Falls, Minn., to capacity.

When somebody moves out of one of the campsites somebody else moves in. Luck in arriving at the right time is the determining factor for the "chosen people."

Two private parks within three miles of the state park catch some of the camper overflow. Some campers go across the river to Traprock Interstate Park in Wisconsin. Park attendants tell turn-aways about all possibilities.

What do the campers do? Some of them just sit.

David DeWitt, 15, of Indianapolis, Ind., was there for a week with his parents. He didn't swim, he said, but he had caught a 5-pound catfish and a 5-pound eel. He didn't eat the eel.

This camp has surfaced roads and other refinements.

The inner circle of campsites is equipped with electric outlets for the campers' equipment. The fee is $1.75 a night with electricity, $1.50 without.

Many campers favor aluminum lawn chairs in which they sit and look at the river. The river is indeed beautiful.

For others there are nature trails. As at other state parks one may take conducted hikes with a naturalist at certain times. The office at the gate has printed schedules.

Many rent canoes and take rides on the excursion boats.

William O'Brien State Park, downstream toward Stillwater, Minn., alternates conducted trail walks with Interstate. There are also "self-guiding" trails at both parks, for which guide leaflets go into much detail about rocks, trees and plants.

*   *   *

An interesting feature of O'Brien Park on the St. Croix above Marine, is Greenberg Island, donated by David S. Greenberg and dedicated in 1961.

The park, itself, is much improved: surfaced roads, beach, refectory, council room with fireplace for groups.

The beach, which has a lifeguard at peak times, is on a sandy pool made by a tributary and held back by a dam a few feet above river level.

You reach 66-acre Greenberg Island by crossing a rock and timber pedestrian bridge, built to withstand floods. The island is quite wild but interlaced with sandy hiking trails.

A small pond in its middle is surrounded by tall broadleaved arrowhead. The roots have a high starch content, and the Indians boiled or roasted them as we do potatoes.

Men in the Lewis and Clark expedition used them as a substitute for bread.

CHAPTER XI WANDERING

Trip No. 63 / Scandia

THOUSANDS OF SUNDAY drivers have taken the scenic trip from Stillwater up Hwy. 95 to Taylors Falls, but relatively few have taken a short jog west off Hwy. 95 on County Rd. 52 at the sign saying "Scandia."

Three miles takes one into the little crossroads town of Scandia, site of what its natives reckon to be the first Swedish settlement in Minnesota and rich in the kind of pioneer Swedish farming history abounding in this area.

Passing Meister's tavern on the right and climbing a slight upgrade to the top of a small hill, one finds, to the right, a big Handy Pantry store, groceries on one side, a candle shop on the other, with terrariums, curios, curio stands and such. This was the old "Commercial Center" of Scandia. Across the street are Elim Lutheran Church and cemetery, Memorial Park and the old parsonage.

Running between the church and cemetery is County Rd. 3, which leads in a couple of miles southward to, on the left, an obelisk monument to the first Swedish settlers (Oscar Roos, Carl Fernstrom, Och August Sandahl, Fran Vestergotland, Bosatte Sig a Detta Hemman), and a bit farther on, straight ahead when the road bends to the right, the old Hay Lake School near which three young Swedes staked a claim in 1850, the beginning of Scandia. Work is going on to turn the old school into a museum.

Scandia, though just a shadow of its once-bustling trade-center self, is full of feeling for the past.

187

The fine brick church building, looking serene and untroubled, is the sixth in a succession. It dates back only to 1930.

The first church, built in 1856, quickly became a schoolhouse. It was succeeded by a second log building in 1861. A third church, a more ambitious structure, 80 by 50 feet with a steeple 80 feet high, went up in 1874.

On Sept. 9, 1884, a tornado totaled church No. 3. Services were held the following Sunday in the midst of the rubble, the pastor preaching from a strangely intact pulpit.

A fourth church, brick veneered, with organ and stained glass, lasted until lightning struck it May 21, 1907. It burned to the ground.

In 1908 a cathedral-like church of brick and masonry with turrets, massive tower, and arched, louvered fenestrations, went up.

On May 30, 1930, fire destroyed church No. 5. A nearby parish hall had wooden steps under which, it was believed, someone tossed a cigarette. The wind was strong.

Church No. 6 now stands proud and strong with an adjacent brick parish hall. Inside one finds two cornerstones, the lower one reading, "1908" and the upper, "Rebuilt, 1930."

The commercial part of Scandia grew from the enterprise of one Frank Lake, who began as a boy house-to-house peddler around Bone Lake, northwest of Scandia. He started a store in Scandia in 1879, and it grew from a shack to a two-story structure with sheds, a barn and other storage areas. Lake even had a water tower in the barn and his own neighborhood waterworks.

After the coming of the automobile, Scandia settled into what it is today, a quiet byway off the main highway with a "Handy Pantry" that was once a super-mercantile, known in the old days as "The Merc."

WANDERING

Trip No. 64 / Up Walker Way

THE FIRST TIME I VENTURED into northern Minnesota's vacationland I felt frustration and disappointment. That was about 1925.

The feeling wore off when my uncle, driving a Model-T Ford and tent trailer, led our two Model-T party to the shores of the first lake on our itinerary. But it had taken the better part of a day to get there,

The fact of the matter is that one can drive his head off around and about some of our lakiest resort regions and very seldom see a lake. What one sees are tiers of signboards with arrows pointing through the woods to choice lakeshore resorts located a mile or so off the highway.

A good many towns in the midst of resort areas have some attractive water adjacent to or running through them, but a good many more do not. Except for the sign boards and sporting goods stores, they might as well be towns anywhere.

Nature is not a publicity man, and even those fortunate towns with lakes and streams in their precincts seldom offer the new visitor the dramatic first impression which his mind's eye has been nurturing through the long dry miles en route.

A while ago I found the first impression which my own private mind's eye had been nurturing. I was driving over a hill going northward on highway 371 from Hackensack, and there it was—Walker, Minn.

The approach to this town from this direction is wide-screen at its best.

You get up on a hill, and suddenly there are the woods, the hills and the town "nestling," as they say. This one really nestles. The water of Leech Lake is sky blue, gem-like and all the rest of it, and the panorama with its interesting irregularities stretches for miles and miles to the horizon.

A glance at the map will prove that Walker is only one of dozens of Minnesota resort centers surrounded by recreational facilities in wonderful profusion. What Walker boasts is an entryway which lifts the viewer to an exceptional vantage point. I'm afraid there isn't much that towns in flat surroundings can do about this except build big ramps and route the highways over them so arriving tourists will get up there and get a good look.

There's something else they can do, though, and that is to provide a landmark which the home movie and camera bugs will photograph. This means more to a resort area than the numbers of satisfied camera hobbyists might suggest, for nearly every one who takes vacation pictures insists on showing them to friends and relatives. Every advertising man knows what this means. It means viewership. It means circulation.

Bemidji, 36 miles northwest of Walker, doesn't have the big hill approach, but it has beautiful lakeshore, a thriving lakeshore tourist center with excursion boat and airplane rides, and a couple of man-made landmarks right smack in the middle of its tourist center. No amateur photographer can resist them, unless he specializes in taking pictures of nothing but wild flowers, old men in parks or skeleton steel against the sky.

I'm talking about Bemidji's concrete statues of Paul Bunyan and his ox, painted blue—and Bunyan's shirt painted red.

These masterpieces aren't by Carl Milles and they aren't chiseled out of Mexican onyx, but they are individualizing.

If you've ever watched many home movies of vacations, you know that after so many lakes and pine trees. you don't know where you are, but the instant you see the aforementioned statues you know, and as long as somebody keeps painting them, the mood will be festive. Not bad identification for any resort center.

WANDERING

Trip No. 65 / Along the Rum

IF YOU LIKE TO PACK a lunch, there are some nice places along the Rum River.

I had my eye on a place called Oxlip, which sounded to me like an interesting name, but on the way there on Hwy. 47 north out of Anoka I was about to slide through St. Francis when I remembered that somebody had advised me to take a look at it.

You might miss it from the highway, but St. Francis is right on the Rum River, and if you go eastward off Hwy. 47, you'll see a place where you can drive down near the water just south of the bridge.

Here the water rushes over the remains of an old mill dam. Well above river level and back toward the village. is a very green "square" with its little antiquated band-

stand. A boy at the supermarket told me they never give concerts there any more. That's a shame.

Just eight miles north of St. Francis, back on Hwy. 47, I turned west and soon was in Oxlip. I found that it consists of one vacant general store which closed in 1955, a Baptist Church which was between ministers, a vacant summer cottage and a neat bungalow occupied by a mechanic who had lived there for some years but never heard how the place got its name.

He pointed out some handsome spruce growing across the road by the summer cottage and told me that the owner told him that he had grown those trees from some seeds that came in a little brown envelope. The trees stood 20 feet tall.

Conifers do well in these Anoka sand plains. Between here and Princeton, as you continue west on the blacktop, you'll notice some handsome stands of young Norway pines which have been planted as windbreaks and as tree farms.

The blacktop runs into Hwy. 169. Here I turned north a mile or two into Princeton, which also stands on the Rum River and has a very nice city park with picnic tables right on the south edge of the Rum near the Hwy. 169 bridge.

Sometime in August I plan to take a good look around Princeton. That's when the flowers are at their best. What flowers? Well the *Princeton Union* ran this notice at the top of Page 1:

"Plan to Plant. Keep Princeton a Flower City."

"It really works," said the Kings, "It's beautiful."

WANDERING

Trip No. 66 / Along the Upper Cannon

THE GLORIES OF MID-JUNE country-style living are visible on a sunny day's tour through the Cannon River towns of Northfield, Faribault and Warsaw, Minn., along Hwys. 3 and 60.

The fields and leafy trees never are greener nor the rivers and lakes fuller. If it came to a beauty contest, never could the charms of southern Minnesota give the pine forests of the north a better run for their money.

The peonies are in all their glory at the Brand Peony Farm on the southeast edge of Faribault.

Archie and Bob Tischler, the owners, are developing new varieties. They've got a seedling, unnamed as yet, that grows like a hedge bush with its rosy red blooms appearing flat across the top.

There are others of interest to connoisseurs—and beauty for everyone—yellows, pinks, poppy-like hybrids and whites with a deep carmine stain in the middle—all luxuriating.

*   *   *

There is also water life along the Cannon. If you have fishing in mind, a good destination is a bridge at the upriver or southeast corner of Cannon Lake.

This is near Warsaw, about 7 miles southwest of Faribault. To get there, leave Faribault on Hwy. 60. From Hwy. 65, measure 2.7 miles and then turn right across the railroad tracks on Rice County Road 12.

This will take you along the edges and across Cannon Lake on a kind of causeway and finally to the bridge. Here I found fishermen lining the bridge and road. Kids swam across the river.

Looking for a fill-in on the place, I turned into "Doc's Dock" by the bridge. I chose wisely.

Doc had cabins and two modest frame buildings, one a motel and the other his headquarters for bait sales, boat rentals, aspirin, straw hats and other small comforts. "Come right in," a sign said. "We just look expensive."

"Doc" (a widower named C. A. Gustafson) stopped to fish this particular junction of Cannon Lake and the Cannon River when he was on a trip with his brother in 1945.

"There was an old wreck of a house standing here," he recalled with a far-away look. He quit the insurance business and bought the land.

One of his "tickets" says: "This is a free coupon. It isn't good for anything but it's free. Come up for the rest of your life at Doc's Dock." That's what Doc did.

"He didn't always have that beard, though," said a straw hat salesman from Red Wing.

"It's so itchy I darned near shaved it off yesterday," Doc said, "but I guess I'll keep it 'til my girl sees it."

*   *   *

Recreational life along the Cannon:

By a waterfall over a dam just upstream from the Hwy. 3 bridge in Faribault, I saw boys swimming and fishing.

At the center bridge in Northfield a Carleton senior aimed a 50-pound fiberglass bow with a heavy fishing arrow at carp below the falls. A line ran from the base of the arrow into a reel on the bow.

"I got a 12-pounder earlier," he said. "The barb broke off the arrow and he fell back in."

WANDERING
Trip No. 67 / Big Lake to Lester Prairie

A DRIVE DOWN HWY. 25 southward from Big Lake, Minn., can be rather inspiring for anyone alert to the need for small town parks and recreational facilities.

First there is Monticello, Minn., on the Mississippi, with two parks on the river, one by the Hwy. 25 bridge and another a few blocks southeast of it. The latter is especially inviting to picnickers with its tall trees and grassy riverbanks.

Another 10-mile hitch down Hwy. 25 brings you to Buffalo, Minn., with its own lakeshore and lakeshore park just a few blocks southeast of the business district. This is another big park with big shade trees. This one has a cottage for Girl Scout activities.

Monticello and Buffalo take further advantage of their waterfront views. Monticello's new hospital overlooks the river southeast of the park. Buffalo has a "Retirement Center" on a knoll above the lakeside park.

As you leave Buffalo and go southward on Hwy. 25 notice the well-kept Buffalo golf course on the right side of the road.

Still farther south on Hwy. 25 we come to Watertown, Minn., with frontage along the Crow River. Here on a sunny morning I found a dozen boys fishing for carp in the rushing water just below a shallow dam.

In the 10 minutes I watched them, Dennis and David

Ferniok (brothers) both caught carp on worms. There aren't many towns that have open shorefishing facilities like this. John Mathews said they also catch bullheads, sunfish and crappies.

To wind up the tour, if you aren't too tired, proceed south on Hwy. 25 to Hwy. 7 and then run west about eight miles to Lester Prairie, Minn., south of the highway. Here is a town without lake or river. That didn't stop the businessmen from putting in a swimming pool that draws swimmers from a wide area.

Lester Prairie is "off the main drag" (south of Hwy. 7 and east of Hwy. 261) but it has been doing a lot more than vegetating in recent years. It has a thriving steel equipment manufacturing plant (the Schwartz Co.), a big lumberyard, other respectable businesses, quite a number of pretty houses and a new school.

Not too different from a lot of other country towns, in fact, and apparently that was the trouble. Its citizens felt the need of a little more zing in their community pride.

They decided to build a swimming pool without borrowing a nickel. Bill McGowan, who came to town to join the Schwartz Co., gave me a run-down on that. He was the finance chairman.

The community wound up with a swimming pool worth $65,000 to $70,000. The cash outlay was something under $40,000, nearly all pledged by contributors. The difference was made up by volunteer labor and contributed materials.

A plumber contributed fixtures for the bathhouse, somebody else gave building blocks for the filter plant and so on.

The L-shaped pool 82.6 by 40 feet one way and 35 by 75 the other way—(12 feet down at the deepest end) went into an 8-acre park containing a baseball diamond (the site of Crow River Valley League games on Sunday afternoons) and other space. Swimming fees make it self-supporting.

WANDERING
Trip No. 68 / East Shore of Lake Pepin

DON'T WRITE OFF the fall colors in late autumn just because they are past their peak. There still can be a lot of mellow comfort in the russet shades and an occasional stimulating flash of aspen gold against the darker background.

This is especially true south of the **Twin Cities**. **In** a ride south along Lake Pepin the rocks, the green cedars, the subdued background leaves, the sky and water are a delight.

Curiosity Satisfied: If you've ever driven Hwy. 35 between Bay City and Maiden Rock, Wis., through a

rustic valley, you must have wondered about a tall red-dish structure covered with reddish dust and crammed between the sandstone bank and the highway.

There is a loading area, and trucks keep running in and out. I stopped to find out what was going on. Joe Rott (pronounced "Roat"), of Bay City, told me.

It's a sand mine owned and run by Earl McCarty and his father before him. It has been there since 1890. The mine's main tunnel goes half a mile into the bank and has over 60 side branches.

The sand comes wet into the big structure by the high-way where it is dried, sifted and separated into different grades. It goes into the trucks in big white 100-pound bags, and there are days when a hundred tons of it leave the mine.

What's it good for? Primarily two things: sand-blast-ing and molds for metal castings.

*   *   *

Before reaching Alma, Wis., below Lake Pepin and the Chippewa and Buffalo rivers, you'll find many pretty wayside lookouts and parking areas, with picnic tables, and Alma, itself, has Buena Vista Park high on the bluff.

However, if you prefer to eat in a restaurant, you'll find plain but excellent fare in the Alma Hotel Cafe. The day I was there they had barley soup, rolls, fresh sliced tomatoes, roast pork or Swiss steak, peas, mashed pota-toes and gravy, coffee or tea and apple pie a la mode.

*   *   *

South of Alma, if you turn west or riverward to Buf-falo City, you'll find an interesting resort and riverside community. Here again the Wisconsin penchant for pleasant parks is altogether praiseworthy.

The ambitious Buffalo Valley Recreation Project, proposed for the beautiful hills and dales between Alma and Cochrane, including the Lester Mueller farm east of Hwy. 35, is abandoned—unfortunately.

WANDERING

Trip No. 69 / Along the Crow

THERE ARE SEVERAL reasons why a drive along the Crow River isn't a bad idea in May, especially if you don't want to drive far.

The trees are not yet fully leafed out, and hence there are longer visible stretches of this interesting winding stream wherever you can see it.

The water, while nowhere near the flood levels marked at Berning Mill during the record flood of 1952 and other high years, still is high enough to make a fine rush going over the dam there and to come up to the banks for bank-fishing at many shady places.

I counted 10 river bank fishermen on a sunny morning's drive upstream along the Crow from Berning Mill to a bit south of Hanover. They were carp fishing. Standing on the south shore across from Berning Mill, Mr. and Mrs. Jim Neumann of New Hope were using corn kernels for bait and said they had had excellent luck a day or two before.

Another nice thing about this northeast-running stream, which forms the boundary between Hennepin and Wright Counties, is that it evidently was a traffic artery in earlier days, and some of the buildings along and near it hark from those earlier days—the mills, of

course, country schoolhouses, and stores and houses with old-fashioned porches. If you are partial to mellow dilapidation, you'll find some of that, too.

A good way is to drive northwest on Hwy. 152 to St. Michael. Before getting there, but within view of the St. Michael watertower, you'll find a blacktop sidespur to the left which takes you just ¼-mile around through Berning Mill and back to St. Michael where a left turn puts you on a county road following the Crow through Hanover to Rockford, where you cross the Crow and continue to follow it to Delano and, if you like, all the way to Watertown.

*   *   *

From Watertown a gravel road will take you to St. Bonifacius and Hwy. 7, or a blacktop road will take you around a square corner to Hwy. 7 and the same end results—a clear shot to Minneapolis.

WANDERING

Trip No. 70 / Cannon Falls to Taylors Falls

THERE IS SOMETHING about running water and fresh air that restores one's belief in summer as a distinct possibility in the future scheme of things, however wet, stinging, or nippy the April winds may turn. And so it was that one crisp April day I set off in search of spring torrents.

The Cannon River was rather dark and turgid where it rushed through the Cannon Falls, Minn., dam, purposely opened so that the fresh spring current would flush it out, but the park below the dam near the center of town was high and dry.

Stop in the off-street parking space and go inside for a look at its unusual modern design. Very interesting. Very functional. There is a feeling of spaciousness around corners all within modest dimensions. The altar, of course, stands free after the new fashion so that the priest may face the congregation.

*   *   *

From Cannon Falls how about going back north on Hwy. 52 and taking the right fork marked "To Hwy. 61" just out of town? This leads north to Hastings (on Hwy. 61). The first roadside cafe on the right near the outskirts as you enter town is exceptionally good if you feel like stopping.

A little farther north, after you cross a small bridge, is the turn-off to the right, marked by a sign, to Mill Park on the Vermillion River across from Hastings State Hospital.

The remains of the mill building, built by Gov. Alexander Ramsey in the early 1800s and later destroyed by fire, are excellent ruins in texture but quite a challenge photographically. There are the tempting contrasts, the rushing water, dangling vines, sand, time-eroded stones, and there is the problem of shooting them without getting drainpipes and other inappropriate items across the river in the background.

*   *   *

If you're ready for some more driving and want to see a waterfall that's really roaring and plunging, head north to Taylors Falls.

A good way is to turn right off Hwy. 61 to Prescott on Hwy. 10 at the top of the hill after crossing the Mississippi northward. Then turn left on a blacktop road by an "Apples" sign near the bottom of the hill descending into Prescott. This will take you north through Afton and Stillwater on Hwy. 95 to Taylors Falls.

The excursion boats do not run there until May 1, but when I was there, the St. Croix, north of town, thundered over the dam, for here the northern snow run-off was being felt.

Bird Note: At this time of year the purple martins send a flying squad into the area to select their nesting houses.

Have your martin houses up with screen on all the doors to keep out sparrows.

When you see the flying squad members return with the flock, take off the screens and the martins will nest. (In the fall clean the houses. If there are any dead birds, you will notice that the swallows have embalmed them).

WANDERING

Trip No. 71 / Last Holiday Weekend

AND THEN THERE's Labor Day, summer's farewell for
most of us. You may want to celebrate it with one of
several tours within an easy drive of the Twin Cities.

Southwest 79 miles on U.S. highway 169 to Mankato

(Sibley Park, Minneopa State Park), return via state highway 60 eastward by Elysian Lake, Waterville, Faribault and state highway 218 north along Cannon River to Northfield. Pastoral scenery.

Picnic in Sand Dunes State Forest, about 40 miles northwest of Minneapolis and approachable either through Zimmerman on U.S. highway 169 or Big Lake on U.S. highway 52. You can swim in Ann Lake in the forest.

For hiking trails, St. Croix State Park. Drive about 85 miles north on U.S. highway 61 to Hinckley and then east on state highway 48. Scenery not spectacular but there are fishing holes in the St. Croix and its tributaries and swimming beaches on the St. Croix. Also, a boat launching site.

State highway 96 (or 36) to Stillwater (privately operated marina for boaters) and state highway 95 to Boomsite (picnic grounds on St. Croix), and William O'Brien State Park (picnic grounds), Interstate Park (picnic and camping) and Taylors Falls (excursion boat rides).

United States highway 12 east to Wisconsin highway 35, south to River Falls, Wis. (swimming pool), Wisconsin highway 29 to Spring Valley (Crystal Cave), Wisconsin 128 to Elmwood, county road T to Eau Galle, county road Z to Downsville, Wisconsin 25 to Menomonie. Rolling verdure all the way.

United States highway 61 southeastward along Minnesota side of Lake Pepin and miles of sandy beach. Swimming. Picnicking. Boating.

*   *   *   *

For something a little more ambitious with an overnight stop along the way, here's a suggested tour bulwarked with facilities.

Roughing it is okay, but sometimes, especially toward

summer's end, it's nice if someone has anticipated your coming and lined up a few things.

Pine River, Minn., is 157 miles north of Minneapolis on U.S. highway 371. Right near the middle of this pretty municipality is a swimming pool behind a dam in piny surroundings. It's a great place for good swimmers and divers—has a steel high-diving tower solidly mounted on concrete at the pool's edge. There's a movie theater in town and lots of resorts in the area.

Venturing nine miles northward along 371 you come to Backus. There aren't many towns of this size with the foresight and thoughtfulness evident on Backus's west border, which happens to be the shore of Pine Mountain Lake.

Here are picnic benches, a lagoon for small boats (with channel marked through shallow water) and a nicely filled-in car turn-around surrounded on three sides by water with sparse rushes and sandy bottom suitable for bathing. In and around the park are willows, golden rod, daisies and gulls.

From here, there is an interesting drive westward along state highway 87 past the Badoura ranger station, between First and Third lakes, through Hubbard to U.S. highway 71 and thence north to Park Rapids.

The latter, of course, is a major resort center. It boasts a municipal beach right in town with spring board, life guards and an area roped off for beginners. Open hours are 1,0 a.m. to noon and 1 to 6 p.m. daily and 1 to 6 p.m. Sundays.

If you still have some steam left, take the 18-mile drive northward to Itasca State Park, between Fish Hook Lake, Portage Lake and miles of woods and roadside wild flowers like purple joe-pyeweed, smooth asters, yellow daisies and golden rod.

If you've ever been to Itasca state park, you know there is enough here to keep an eager tourist busy for one, two or three weeks, depending on his appetite for woodland trails, fishing, Indian lore and nature study.

The park has all kinds of overnight facilities—camp grounds, cabins, multiple houses, lodges. The indoor facilities are at the south end of Lake Itasca and the camp grounds are at the north end.

CHAPTER XII   AFLOAT

Trip No. 72 / On Rainy Lake

Lee Kuluvar runs Northernaire Floating Lodges on Rainy Lake.

Kuluvar's idea for a floating lodge vacation just about floored me.

The beauty of the scenery, of course, is staggering to anybody—the blue water often walled in by flat, angular and sometimes jagged black volcanic rock, the racy squalls that sometimes furrow the water and send its blue ridges dashing and foaming against these black obstacles, the assorted waterfowl (we saw ducks, cranes, gulls, loons and a goose), and above all the sunlight in the pines and other greenery along the water's edge.

But that isn't all that's staggering. The idea of being turned loose with a 30-by-40-foot houseboat to pilot hither, thither and yon among islands, reefs and passes, seemed pleasant and relaxing in anticipation.

But when Don Trompeter, a guide who writes novels, took us eight miles out of port, towing the base camp speedboat, and left us in a place called Lost Bay, my subconscious began whistling a different tune.

As the speedboat reared back and surged out of view with our guide, I tried a brief review of instructions. Keep red buoys to the south, black ones to the north, tie up in a storm, tie up at night, depress the throttle while shifting, don't try to turn too sharply, run the outboard from the rear if the controls go out at the helm and empty the chlorinated toilet once a day.

It looked like adventurous times ahead. Here are some of the things that happened:

I landed a northern while trolling on a mission of sanitation.

Later we cruised to Steamboat Island, an ideal picnic and swimming spot two miles out in the lake. Had a great time, but on the return I bungled starting the engine, broke the throttle control and averted blowing across the lake to Canada only by hooking on to a rocky reef.

The fact that anyone with my lack of outboard motor knowledge could hand-start the motor and get to safe harbor (my son worked the throttle in the rear while I steered up in front) probably is pretty good evidence of certain basic mechanical virtues in these floating lodges.

The second morning found us fogbound, but the afternoon was sunny. Kuluvar, who bought a plane and learned to fly it so he can keep tab on where his lodges are floating, landed in our bay. He delivered two cartons of milk which we had forgotten and fixed the broken control.

On the last evening, too late to head for port, my son dislocated his wrist and factured a hand bone while pole vaulting from ship to shore. We put a splint on the wrist, fed him aspirin all night and cruised back to headquarters, a four-hour trip, in the morning. I am proud to say that I changed gas tanks without stopping the motor. That night a big thunderstorm cut loose, but we were in a motel and our pole vaulter was in International Falls hospital with his arm in a cast.

Lee Kuluvar is an interesting, energetic, ambitious and highly imaginative resort operator. He has a slight liability—passengers like me. I rammed the dock on my final landing.

AFLOAT

Trip No. 73 / On the Namakagon

I WENT CANOEING HEAD over heels down the Namakagon River in northern Wisconsin one September.

The last previous time I had paddled a canoe was about 20 years before—on a lake. I never in my life had heard of a "whitewater man" (a paddler who is hep to churning water).Wally Peterson told me to leave my wallet, watch and camera in the car. I wondered why. It was a sunny day. Beautiful. The river looked lazy.

Tony Wise, who owns Mt. Telemark and outfits canoers at Historyland (Hayward, Wis.), had invited some fellow ski-area operators and friends of skiing to paddle his canoes down the Namakagon.

Historyland offers the tourist a Chippewa Indian village, a heavily equipped logging camp-museum and a logging camp cook shanty restaurant with authentic decorations, table settings and cuisine. In the placid water nearby are the blackened stumps of an old logging railroad loading platform.

In these authentic surroundings I heard Peterson of Trollhaugen, Oscar Cyr of Pine Bend, Pete Dennison of Norski Hill and Jimmy Johnston, Theodore Wirth ski school head, ski area operator and golfer, debating whether we should shoot the dam.

"Aren't you afraid you'll drag on the bottom?" Peterson asked Johnston, who is a big man.

"I debated this matter with myself a long time before I decided to come," Johnston admitted. "Let's shoot the dam. You notice how everybody is pairing up without me?"

At the launching site near Cable the experts put the greenhorns in the bows. Johnston got Peterson for a stern man, and I drew Oscar Cyr, an old whitewater man from New England.

The fact that our bows outweighed our sterns was considered immaterial. We shoved off with our bows plowing deeply.

"They're going downhill," Dennison observed. "We'll never keep up."

They did, however, manage to keep up with us, mostly by staying ahead. Shady overhangs full of bushes, balsam, spruce and white pine coasted by, tops in the sun. In places where rocks were close to the surface the shiny swift water bent, dented and rippled.

Peterson slapped the sides of his canoe and did some Indian chanting. Ben Van Sant, ski lift salesman, kept saying, "It's only a four-foot drop over the dam," with jovial intent. Everybody guyed Johnston even though he and Peterson majestically averted bumping bottom most of the time.

Johnston retaliated by singing like the Ink Spots and cracking jokes like "I can canoe, can-oo?"

This went on for about 10 charming, scenic miles until, feeling tempered by the swift waters and a few bumps on the rocks, I found us approaching the afore-mentioned dam at the end of a narrow lake.

This rugged little structure had a spillway of sorts at the left, half clogged with logs so that the water seemed to descend in steps. One log paralleling the runway on the right had a series of railroad spikes sticking up about five inches along its topside, which was half out of the water.

Peterson, having steered the Peterson-Johnston craft up to the right of the dam to look it over, hollered, "Keep to the right!"

There were three other canoes kind of marking time, so Oscar, my whitewater stern man, said, "Let's go," and away we went, a little too far to the right, ran up on the spiked log about half way down the spillway, caught our bow on one of the spikes and flipped. I mean really flipped.

Suddenly we were bumping around among the submerged logs, and the mercifully light aluminum canoe was bumping around on our heads. The whitewater in the spillway was wrapping my whitewater stern man around one of the logs, his stomach in the middle and his head and legs forming the ends of a horseshoe.

I was discommoded in several ways that remain vague in my memory, but later I discovered a bruised leg, a sore rib and a stiff neck.

The rest of the party looked on with an air of extreme interest.

"Nobody was laughing," Jimmy told me later, "because the situation was a little touchy."

However, Whitewater Cyr and I pulled ourselves up on the spiked log, emptied Wise's excellent, light canoe and floated down the rest of the descent without incident.

It was somewhat humiliating to watch the rest of the party make the run with no trouble at all. One pair did it twice so Bob Hadden, a commercial artist and ski photographer, could take pictures of them.

They all went back to look for my old cotton pants,

which had been in the canoe bottom (I was wearing swimming shorts). The pants wouldn't have been worth looking for except that they had my car keys in them.

During the search several things happened. Pete Dennison rolled up his trouser legs so he wouldn't get wet and stepped off a drop-off up to his chest. Wally Peterson got out to help in the hunt.

Jimmy Johnston recorded the historic event on movie film until a rock flipped his canoe. With great presence of mind he sank up to his neck while holding his camera aloft like the Statue of Liberty. His dry straw hat stayed on his head and his teeth clenched a cigar three or four inches above the swirling surface.

"Get the camera!" the excited party cried.

"Give me a light," requested Johnston with a fine sense of the dramatic.

The real hero of the occasion, however, was Dennison. While I was urging the searchers to give up, Dennison pushed inexorably up the rushing spillway. "I can find anything," he insisted. So-saying he reached down until the water was rushing around his chin and brought up the dripping trousers. The keys still were in the pocket.

After a dry change, a great dinner at Historyland and an entertaining solo by Ray Conrad, skiing guitarist, we started a return, by easy stages, to the Twin Cities. At the last stage, 9 p.m., the kidders still were joshing Johnston.

"It all adds up to one thing," he said. "I'm big. I'm going on a diet tomorrow."

"Tell me one thing," said Peterson. "Did you get that straw hat because Sammy Snead wears one like it?"

"I don't believe that deserves an answer," said Johnston.

AFLOAT

Trip No. 74 / On the Mississippi

I HAD FUN ON this one. Not only was my curiosity satisfied but I shared in an adventure.

The greatest thing I saw was a bald eagle (that's right, an American eagle), a truly magnificent bird, sitting on a treetop near the water's edge, the first I've seen out of captivity.

Dennis Raedeke, Taylors Falls, Minn., excursion boat pilot, catfishing guide and ski instructor, invited me to take a ride up the river one recent spring when he and his father-in-law, Bob Muller, president of the Muller Boat Co. at Taylors Falls, went to get a new excursion boat, the *Kathy M,* under construction in the Whitaker boat works at Winona, Minn.

Bob and Dennis started upriver from Winona. At 6 a.m. I joined the rest of the crew (Curtis Liljenberg, Taylors Falls; Paul Johnson, 1100 E. County Road C, St. Paul; Kathy Muller, Bob's daughter and the boat's namesake, and Mary Ann Swenson, Taylors Falls, at Stillwater.

Bob's wife rode south with us on Wisconsin Hwy. 35 to bring back the car. At Fountain City we spotted the *Kathy M* tooling upriver and got aboard.

The *Kathy M,* destined to become a handsome excursion boat with canopy and old-fashioned steamer-type ornamentation, at this point was a strange craft—a 7-ton open steel hull with twin 140-horsepower V-8 engines in back and a shiny pilot's wheel and control panel in front. Between these lay about 30 feet of flooring with a tent pitched in the middle. Passengers' visibility—unlimited.

The engines could lift the prow and make the boat "plane" on its two longitudinal ridges at about 12 m.p.h. Top speed, 25. Break-in speed, 8 to 15. It was being broken in.

The excitement of the maiden voyage, following the charts, watching the red and black river markers (keep Red to your Right when Returning from sea) and going through the locks kept everyone on his feet a good share of the time.

Above Alma we saw the eagle, about 100 yards upstream of the 755.1 distance marker. Dennis nudged me and handed me the glasses. The bird's profile, with its big hooked beak and snowy head and neck feathers, was proud, still and erect against the blue sky above the treetop. Its nest, nearby in the same tree, looked like a small haystack. Before anyone could aim a camera, the bird spread its wings and lifted out of the tree. Soon up a side valley a mate joined it, and we saw the two of them soar and repeatedly switch positions in the sky.

AFLOAT

Trip No. 75 / On the Lower Cannon

THE PEOPLE ALONG the lower Cannon River valley have been waking up to the exciting hand that nature has dealt them.

Properly handled, it could be a recreational bonanza.

First, there is the valley scenery, the little farms, the winding waterway, and the high hills with their grass carpeting, their clumpy cedars and their sandstone patchwork that seem to cut off the outside world.

The atmosphere seizes a visitor with an urge to settle down and forget his responsibilities.

*   *   *

In the middle of it all nestles the little settlement of Welch (one store, one tavern, one post office, one creamery and one feed mill) 3 miles south of Hwy. 61 between Hastings and Red Wing.

Until recently, the only consciously cultivated recreation in Welch centered around the carefully built regulation horseshoe pitching courts on the town side of the bridge across from Mrs. Earl Montey's Cannon River Inn.

Here, led by Ed Kruse, the Welch horseshoe sharpshooters matched skill with Wastedo, Oxford, Waterford, Northfield, Faribault, Stanton and Randolph, often won, and still do.

Then Gib Axelson started his Hidden Valley Camp

Ground on 300 acres along the river's south side just upstream from Welch. Next came the Welch Village Ski Area and Richard Scrivner's Welch Riding Stables.

It's all native enterprise. Axelson works in a Red Wing

tanning plant. Scrivner, Axelson's brother-in-law, works at the Red Wing Training School for Boys. Clem and Leigh Nelson, the ski area owners, are sons of Clarence Nelson, the Welch grain and feed mill owner.

All three recreational enterprises, camping, riding, and skiing, are winning fast acceptance from patrons outside the area.

*   *   *

Now comes a new kick—canoeing down the Cannon.

Notices in valley newspapers attracted 16 canoeloads. Clarence Krech and son Steve, of Farmington, saw a notice in the *Dakota County Tribune*. Krech, a veteran of some Root River canoe trips, said, "When I see one of those notices, I take off."

Gish Gisleson and Lane Welcome, Faribault painters, were going canoeing anyway, and joined the group for the first leg of the journey. They proved to be a lively addition. They rolled over in rapids near the start and again while shooting the dam at Welch, but that was on their second run. They enjoyed it so much that they did it three times and made it twice.

When I caught up with them they were in Mrs. Montey's Cannon River Inn between runs two and three.

At the campgrounds, a strong Red Wing-Cannon Falls contingent gathered around a long picnic table.

*   *   *

While the canoer-campers relaxed, Gib Axelson kept running his tractor to clear and grade some more camp-sites. Every year he adds a few improvements. Nature has helped him by cutting a corner in the river channel and leaving a nice sand and gravel island for swimmers. "I was going to build a swimming pool, but now I guess I won't need it," Gib said.

*   *   *

Most of the Red Wing and Cannon Falls canoers finished the trip the next day, although some dropped out. It poured rain, and a stiff wind forced most of the party, including the Nelson brothers, to cross the Mississippi at the Cannon outlet, which is swampy, and land on the Wisconsin side.

Clyde Ryberg, veteran canoer and small-boat sailor, admitted that he got lost where the Cannon nears the Mississippi and becomes "sort of a dismal swamp." Some markers are planned, and then it will be better.

AFLOAT
Trip No. 76 / On the Apple River

THE EARLY SEPTEMBER sun was bright and I couldn't resist it. I floated down the Apple River on an inner tube.

On land or afloat I daresay there isn't a more refreshing mile of travel in the United States than this wet little marine excursion from Somerset, Wis., to a pickup point a mile downstream.

It appeals equally to the senses of sight, sound and touch. This innocent and delightful form of recreation has been written up and photographed, locally and nationally, so many times since Cedric Adams gave it a journalistic send-off in 1938 that if there is anything more that I can say, it's simply that it's fun in September, as well as mid-summer, if you pick a warm day and like water with a little zing to it.

Dave Breault (pronounced "Broe"), proprietor of the

Terrace night club and restaurant, told me that on a good Sunday he outfits four to five hundred inner tube floaters. On the side of his parking lot nearest the river he has a

masonry tile building divided into two dressing rooms for quick changes into swim suits.

Standard advice is to wear some kind of old shoes or tennis shoes so you won't hurt your feet on the rocks whenever you want to wade or stand up to readjust.

The water moves briskly, and the inner tube imparts a swinging circular motion, almost hypnotic in its effect. Branches overhang the stream, which is shallow enough for wading all the way to the pickup point, where Breault has stretched a chain across the stream and on the left bank helpfully has tacked up a sign pointing at the chain reading, "Chain."

The chain gives you a handy way to pull into shore and reminds you that if you go beyond, you'll have to walk back. Also, there's deep water beyond.

The banks are quite high. The patches of long-needled white pine, the leafy "bridges" through which you float from shade into sunlight, the gravelly and stony bottom, sometimes alive with bright green underwater plant life waving in the current, the lulling motion and the ripples near the banks where the stream is swiftest combine to make it quite a ride.

Sometimes when you're sitting and get into the quieter shallower parts of the river, your stern may run aground. Thing to do is straighten out, head back and feet forward —great for the stomach muscles. If this doesn't do it, there's only one solution. Get up and wade back into deeper water.

If the sun gets warm on your face, just lean back, hold your nose, dip your head under water and let the cool Apple River recondition you. If the inner tube pops out while you're trying this, you'll have to get on your feet and go plopping after it, but don't fret. It's all part of the general Apple River plan for circulation restoration.

If you're looking for more action and a change of scenery, both are to be found upriver. John J. Raleigh, owner of the upstream River's Edge restaurant and nightclub, has rented inner tubes to as many as five thousand floaters in a warm week.

They come in cars, wagons and buses. Many are church groups. A lot of them pick a choice section of river and float it again and again by carrying their inner tubes back upstream and repeating.

Some try standing on them. Most lie down. Some float (or portage, depending on the depth and speed of the water) the upper and lower rapids on either side of the Somerset bridge. Some park their inner tubes by the lower rapids and try jumping into a deep hole by the old dam.

AFLOAT

Trip No. 77 / Small Sailboats

HAVING RIGGED VARIOUS bedsheet rowboat and canoe sails in my youth, having survived a minor canoe-sailing upset with Dennis Raedeke on the St. Croix millpond above Taylors Falls dam, having always had a hankering for home-grown, wind-powered locomotion, I was intrigued by what I saw while driving through Lake City, Minn., recently.

On the Lake Pepin beach eight people were busy with four small sailboats that were not much larger than the canoes and rowboats I had monkeyed with as a boy. Something, a kind of experimental look about the people, made me stop.

What were they up to? Somehow I felt that life was passing me by. They seemed to be doing what I had always wanted to do—learning to sail trim little two-man boats, employing all the sailing techniques that I wanted to master, the same techniques that are applied to fill graceful sails around the world.

These were not homemade boats; but they were about the size and genre of my own craft of fond memory.

Queries led me to Ervin Schmidt, a Rochester, Minn., IBM man and Red Cross safety instructor in small-boat sailing. Somebody had hit upon this excellent idea for an educational, sunny summer afternoon, and he was in charge—surely the envy of every red-blooded typewriter-puncher.

Further envious snooping took me to his students,

226

other Rochester sailors: John Howell, industrial security man, and his wife Angela; the Rev. Warner Davidson, Rochester Methodist Hospital chaplain, wife Ruth, children Jackie and Tom, and others.

The Davidsons owned their boat, a fiber-glass "day-sailor-sloop." Others used light boats supplied by the Red Cross. There had been seven weeks of dry sessions at Rochester Community College. Now they were having four weeks of water sessions.

Reflecting upon Lake City, I investigated further and found, as often before, that it pays to look beyond the end of one's nose. My inquiries led me to Kurt Vos, aquatic supervisor of the Minneapolis Park Board.

He said that the same sort of small-boat sailing instruction goes on in Minneapolis; the Park Board started doing it in 1970. They had about 50 students the first year. By 1975 they instructed 395.

"Yes," he said, "our sailing program has really taken off in about the last three years. It wasn't until last year that we bought our own boats for it. . . ."

"We're expanding into some weekend lessons," Vos said. "So we can use boats more on weekends and also to see if this can take care of more people. We're also experimenting with just an hour and a half fundamental course—on weekends, too."

227

CHAPTER XIII
LAKE SUPERIOR

Trip No. 78 / The North Shore

MOST OF MY LIFE, off and on, I've been driving up the North Shore.

Now that I've done it for about the 20th time, I know I'll never get tired of it.

Some friends, recently returned, asked if I had ever walked up the Cascade River. I thought I must have, but on this trip I stopped to make sure.

A path led me up the west side of the river, across a footbridge and back down the east side. I still don't know whether I ever did it before, but today it's one of the most beautiful short walks open to bipeds.

It is important during the tourist season to get an early start and make an early stop or else have reservations, assuming you aren't camping. I prefer the early-stop method, 2 or 3 p.m. That gives you plenty of time to use your sponge rubber soles on the shore boulders, feed the gulls, take a picture, lie flat on your back, listen to the water against the rocks and let your mind off the leash.

The danger of not stopping early is that there might be too many "no vacancy" signs hanging around. There are some fancy resorts and motels along the shore, but you are missing half the fun if you don't spend at least one night in a little old cabin near the water.

There are a lot of them for rent. Some look like wood-sheds sitting out in the sun without a shade tree. Don't worry. The lake breeze comes through cool and clean. I have never found a bad one. They come equipped with the same shoreline, the smooth worn stones, the thick mossy traprock, the thick thimbleberry growths and the bleached driftwood.

Also with kitchen equipment. You're missing half the fun if you don't buy groceries for breakfast, at least, to eat by the window with the view, shimmering or storm-tossed—both great. Nature's own Cinerama.

The drive up the shore was easy despite three short detours. Had some good fresh blueberry pie at a fine old tea room just beyond the Dodge Cabins.

The divided highway extends only to Two Harbors. Planners cite 1985 as the earliest possible extension date.

The George Nelsons, Sr. and Jr., have expanded the lakeshore lodge and added a lot of luxury touches at Lutsen.

Grand Marais is always picturesque, always full of interest and activity.

The art colony is still going strong under Byron Bradley of the Kilbride-Bradley gallery and Birney Quick, teacher at the Minneapolis School of Art.

The school, an old white frame church building, is full of active easels. Quick is also working on a 39-foot mural in St. John's Catholic Church.

In the yard by the school stands a kiln. Bradley built it for ceramics work six years ago.

Cook County Historical Society now has a museum in what was the Grand Marais lighthouse keeper's house until 1946. There's an old pair of scrolled cross-country skis on display that I wanted to steal. Grand Marais was a "popular Indian village" in 1658, according to the museum's history. In 1823 John Jacob Astor had 100 fur traders there and at Grand Portage.

Feeding gulls on the lakefront were 23 male bicyclers between the ages of 15 and 17. They had peddled all the way around Lake Superior and were heading back for Minneapolis. Their leader, Larry Anderson, Youth for Christ high school campus life club director for the Twin Cities area, hails from Grand Marais. His parents own the lakeshore fish house where the boys were stopping. The Andersons gave them a fish dinner.

Cyclists' round-trip distance: 1,300 miles. Casualties to Grand Marais: none. One boy got a headache and took a breather on the supply truck. Weather: only one day without rain, some of it heavy. Boys wore shorts, sweatshirts, no rain gear—got wet and dried off as they peddled. A truck carried the sleeping bags. The group spent one night indoors at Port Arthur YMCA.

Stopping at Tofte, 8 miles below Lutsen on the way back, I found Edgewater Inn owner Thomas Hansen in a selling mood, after 32 years of inkeeping. He said that if he sold the long rambling waterfront motel, dining room, bar and store, he'd be willing to go on working there half-days, "but I'd want two months off each year."

At Duluth I took the two-hour harbor excursion boat-ride and enjoyed it—the first hour more than the second. It afforded an excellent view of Duluth and a few exotic kicks as we churned past ships from Germany, Sweden, Italy and Greece.

LAKE SUPERIOR
Trip No. 79 / The South Shore

PARTS OF UPPER MICHIGAN are as accessible to Minnesotans as parts of Minnesota.

No invidious comparisons are intended. Minnesota's North Shore of Lake Superior is unmatched, but so are stretches of Upper Michigan's South Shore.

They are not exclusive addictions. One can be addicted to both. The vice can be versa.

They are simply different. Well, for one thing, there is the rock-walled austerity of the Minnesota shore that contrasts so beautifully with its cozy, little coves. Much of the Michigan shore, on the other hand, is lined with sand dunes.

For another, the water somehow manages to match the two different moods with its currents and their temperatures. You can swim at Copper Harbor, Mich., on the northernmost point of the South Shore, when a similar dip in the rockbound waters due west on the North Shore could turn you blue.

*   *   *

Beach parties, family-style and otherwise, dominate the scene along a particular stretch of Michigan's South Shore on the Keweenaw Peninsula between Eagle River and Copper Harbor. The road here is Hwy. 26 (Sand Dunes Dr.).

Many tourists bring their own accommodations in the form of tents and campers to this copper country. There are picnic tables on the sand. I found one camping family, grilling hamburgers on a picnic table while their children waded in the lake.

On another stretch of sand three girls and their mothers were rockhunting. A number of "agate shops" along the way attest to the area's popularity with rock hounds.

Occasionally the road leaves the shore to dip into deep, ferny woods and crosses brooks which run into the lake.

*   *   *

Copper Harbor, the end of the trail except for Ft. Wilkins State Park a mile beyond, is an airy little resort town with a variety of motels and eating places, many of them near the water.

The small harbor is a passenger-boat terminal (no cars carried) for Isle Royale National Park headquarters across the lake near the Canadian border. Another terminal is at Minnesota's Grand Portage, which is much closer to the Michigan island than is Michigan.

There is swimming, good eating and abundant lake gazing at Copper Harbor.

*   *   *

Ft. Wilkins State Park embraces the Copper Harbor light house, a reconstructed Ft. Wilkins and Lake Fanny Hooe, named for the sister of an early commanding officer. She disappeared mysteriously.

One of the fort's restored buildings contains a small wildlife museum whose wild flower exhibit includes, for each specimen, not only a drawing, description and pressed flower, but a fresh cut flower standing in water so the viewer can see exactly what it looks like.

Copper Harbor was a boom town during the copper rush that peaked in 1848. There are visible remains of the boom days. One of Michigan's earliest newspapers, the *Lake Superior News and Mining Journal,* started there in 1846., Ft. Wilkins, whose history is as peaceful as Ft. Snelling's, was established to protect the miners from the Indians.

*   *   *

The most spectacular drive on the upper Keweenaw Peninsula is not along the lakeshore but inland on a highway paralleling the aforementioned Sand Dunes Dr.

234

(Hwy. 26) between Copper Harbor and Eagle River.

It is called Brockway Mountain Dr., and you find it by taking Hwy. 26 across Hwy. 41 out of Copper Harbor and then bearing left at the Brockway sign.

Almost immediately, two-thirds of the way up the first steep ascent, one gets a panoramic view of Copper Harbor, Ft. Wilkins, Lake Fanny Hooe and the light house.

Thereafter the up-and-down 15-mile drive repeatedly takes one to 700 feet above Lake Superior level and magnificent views of lake and forest.

Going both ways, up and down the peninsula, one passes through Houghton, named after Douglass Houghton, whose 1840 mineral surveys encouraged the early prospectors.

Houghton is very industrial-looking, and at times congested, but it has the down-at-the heels, old fashioned nostalgia of all faded mining towns plus a hillside charm of its own.

LAKE SUPERIOR

Trip No. 80 / Bayfield

THERE ARE SO MANY interesting reasons for visiting Bayfield, Wis. (and when the apples are in season, there is an extra one) that the best reason seldom is mentioned.

The best reason is that you don't need any reason. Bayfield is one of the finest places imaginable for doing nothing at all.

There is always something to occupy one's attention

along its shore — not grab it, but simply occupy it in a casual, desultory way.

It is a rare quality, a kind of spiritual balm, which allows one to revel in inactivity, to rest, to "forget" and revivify, cell by cell, in the manner of a turtle basking in the sun with one lazy eye open.

      *   *   *

Grand Marais, Minn., is another town like this. Artists gravitate toward both places. Bayfield has a *L'Atelier* Summer Art Gallery, a little old house with a porch reaching to the sidewalk.

Inside one finds a variety of wood prints, etchings, paintings, weldings, tanned fur pelts, hand wrought jewelry, what not.

Much of the work reflects the locale. I found a youth with a little chin spinach in attendance. A phonograph played rock 'n' roll. A small boy played with a toy tractor on the front porch.

*   *   *

The area has about as much antiquity to offer as any place in the Midwest. A nearby French trading post was a thriving settlement when George Washington was a boy. It is believed possible that Etienne Brule came to the region two years before the Pilgrims landed at Plymouth Rock.

Browsing in the Madeline Island Historical Museum, buying apples, and taking boat rides around the Apostle Islands are nice bonuses, but the big thing is just being there, sitting in the park, overlooking the harbor comings and goings, or walking up on a hundred gulls clustered on the breakwater to see them fly.

*   *   *

I am one of many, I'm sure, who mourned the passing of the old Bayfield Inn when it burned down a few years back. I enjoyed some cozy winter nights in the old colonial white frame building with the crystalized harbor outside my window, the boats frozen in the ice, the airplane prop-driven ice taxi carrying the mail to Madeline Island.

I wasn't too happy to see the old ridge-roofed inn replaced by a flat-roofed sandy-hued brick and tile structure that seemed more appropriate for the Mediterranean than Lake Superior. However, my hostile thoughts having proved unequal to the task of removing it, I availed myself of its comforts during my last visit, and I am reconciled. There is much to be said for solid, soundproof masonry, broad windows, and taking one's food and drink in elegance.

*　　　*　　　*

Let's hope that urban renewal won't sweep through the whole town of Bayfield, however — especially the waterfront. The blackened unpainted framework of the old icehouse skidway, a perfect contrast for the white feathered gulls sitting on it, the many-masted yacht basin — such things should be defended.

Boatsmen stop here just to look. While I was watching a variety of craft come and go, a beautiful cabin cruiser from Duluth docked. Owner Erling Hansen, Kenneth Holmgren, Charles Landstrom and Carl Finnay were on their way to Copper Harbor farther up the shore.

Hansen said this was his third boat and the biggest so far (twin Corvette marine engines), which bore out something I had heard; when you trade, you always get a bigger one.

His friends were full of admiration for some water erosion tunnels they had come through along the sand-rock cliffs to the northwest and equally interested in touring the harbor and yacht basin.

*　　　*　　　*

It's kind of a kick to drive your car on the ferry and ride over to Madeline.

This island has a lot of history behind it. It was an Indian headquarters with some religious significance before the explorers got here. Near the landing is a stockade museum, and up the road a piece is Chateau Madeleine, an old mansion turned into a hotel.

Capt. Howard Russell, owner of the ferry *Gar-How II,* gave me a map of the island with his schedule on it and points of interest duly noted.

The affable captain can tell you a good deal about the locale. His mother came there as a girl. He also can fill you in on the economics of ferry boat operation. He

238

runs summer and winter. When the freeze comes, usually in December, he just gets out the airsled.

*   *   *

If you like good thick hamburgers, you'll get one in Bayfield at the place half way up the block on the right as you leave the dock.

LAKE SUPERIOR
Trip No. 81 / Pigeon River High Falls

ON THE UNITED STATES side the road takes you through a high rock cut, straight as an arrow through rock walls about 100 feet high.

Once you are through, the beautiful misty blue-green panorama of Lake Superior and its wooded shore is spread out for you like a fancy tablecloth. September and October leaves emblazon the pattern.

This road leads straight through the northeast tip of Minnesota into Canada.

On the Canadian side of the Pigeon River bridge, the road is connected to the west, perhaps a quarter of a mile from the bridge, with a narrow "High Falls Road" (hand-lettered sign) leading to a parking area from which one may walk.

You walk and climb, mostly climb, and "at your own risk," the sign says, for a look at the thunderous, frightening Pigeon River High Falls — really twin falls divided by big rock slabs and skirted on the north by an old logging sluiceway.

I hadn't seen the falls since I was a boy and was prepared to find them somewhat diminished by time, along with the "giant" snows of yesteryear and other phenomena which have a way of shrinking and becoming less impressive as one grows older.

Not so, the High Falls.

CHAPTER XIV   BYWAYS

Trip No. 82 / Centerville Shore Fishing

THE ICE HAD gone out of the larger lakes, but it had taken a while for the air to pick up the stimulus, the scent.

The main thing is for the rawness to go out of the wind and the mildness to steal in. A little sunshine doesn't hurt, either. The feeling has to work its way through the pores in the skin.

Then, of course, it helps when the docks start to go up. The soaked posts and planks have a subtle smell that is caught best on a still day and arouses all the water-front impulses and awakens all the images — the dreams of glory amid the ripples, the swells or the whitecaps that leave weedy foam along the beach.

*   *   *

Some are more susceptible than others. It's easy to tell who they are. You find them earliest by the water's edge. One fresh April morning "Skip" Johnson, wintertime ski instructor, was raking a hedge by his father's boat works on the west side of White Bear Lake.

Dave Blommer and Butch Casper were installing a dock at nearby Tally's Anchor Inn (boats and bait).

While they worked, two boys were drawn by the hammering. One said, "I caught lots of sunfish right here last summer." He pointed at the shallow water between the dock boards.

*   *   *

243

Westward along Hwy. 96, despite "No Parking" signs and the St. Paul Water Works park's still being closed, young fishermen were dropping lines where the water rushes under the highway southward into Sucker Lake.

North along the flowage winding 20 miles through flatlands, largely isolated, I was sure I would find fishermen west of Centerville between Centerville Lake and Lake Peltier.

I found about 15 fishing there on both sides of the narrows. The water was high and the fish were small, but the ones I saw were bullheads, which in April are at their best for eating.

Across the narrows on a blanket by Centerville Lake Mrs. Richard Nisley fished with her daughter, Marcey Lynn, soon to have a birthday.

"I'll be this old," said Marcey. She tucked in her thumb and held up four fingers. She had weeds on her hook, and her mother had a bullhead which she was waiting for her husband to take off the hook as soon as he got back from the other side of the narrows.

It was Marcey's first fishing trip. "Are you trying to fish for anything in particular?" I asked her mother.

"Anything," she said.

BYWAYS

Trip No. 83 / Tour to Get Lost On

TOUR TO GET LOST ON (not recommended if rain is threatened): You might find a couple of specimens for your photographic collection of aging structures, some rapidly mellowing and some in the falling apart stage.

Directions: Take Hwy. 65 north to Grandy, Minn., five miles north of Cambridge, and turn right or east on Isanti County Road 6, to Rush City on Hwy. 61.

Coming into Rush City, you will notice on the left an old Victorian house with turrets among tall spruce and shade trees.

From Rush City go north on Hwy. 61 and then east across the St. Croix River on Hwy. 70.

You'll find a park on the Wisconsin side. From here, if you feel adventurous, try to follow the river southward as closely as possible on country roads. In this sandy area I found butterfly weed in late July and a beautiful falling-down barn.

Some of the roads have "roller-coaster" ups and downs, much sand and some grass growing in the middle.

This is no place to get caught in a rainstorm. You'd

probably get stuck in one of the hollows. You may see deer, get lost, and even be happy to see a beer can as evidence that somebody has been in here and found his way out.

You'll probably wind up at Wolf Creek, Wis., not far west of Hwy. 87, which will take you south into St. Croix Falls.

BYWAYS

Trip No. 84 / Taylors Falls Library

RECENTLY, NOVELIST THOMAS GIFFORD wrote a thriller, *The Wind Chill Factor,* about a bizzare worldwide Nazi conspiracy in which a key figure was a librarian and a key setting her strange little antique of a library in Coopers Falls.

Coopers Falls, it was later acknowledged, was fashioned after Taylors Falls and the library after the Taylors Falls Library.

The dramatic advantages are apparent—the contrast between the quiet and quaint little library setting and the blood-and-thunder action—the librarian murdered, the library demolished.

An intriguing question is how this library came into being. Old-fashioned library buildings are common enough, but this one is smaller, cuter, fustier looking and has its own special obstinacy against the inroads of change.

Inside, it isn't all that fusty—rather elegant, in fact.

246

And with a glowing book collection. But to the glancer
driving by, it looks more like a relic than a functional arm
of the common cause. Looking incongruously small, about
15 by 30, it sits up there at the head of its nine concrete
steps with their iron pipe rails and just seems to be letting
the world go by.

How did this little architectural entity, strange enough
to capture a novelist's imagination, happen?

In the early years, Taylors Falls had a Young Men's
Literary Society, and in 1854, say the Taylors Falls Library records, the young men started talking about starting a library.

In a few years, one of the local preachers, the Rev.
A. M. McGowan, led a meeting at which a Taylors Falls
Library Association was formed as provided by an 1857
act of the State Legislature. The association acquired

247

books and for a while lending headquarters moved from one store to another, among them Jacob Folsom's, which stood about where Rivard's oil station now is, uphill from the Hwy. 8 bridge.

That was three years after the present library building had been built—as a tailor's shop and residence for one John Jacob Spengler.

The building was remodeled and occupied in 1887. At that time the association had 1,075 volumes. The library has about 7,000 today. The remodeling was thorough and expert. Fine woodwork. Hardwood. Each notch for the adjustable shelves hand-sawed. A half-story attic became a vaulted ceiling. Later, around the turn of the century, the gingerbread work was added to the outside.

BYWAYS

Trip No. 85 / Sleepy Eye

THE GOLDEN GATE to Fun Ski Area is reached by driving six miles north of Sleepy Eye on Hwy. 4, turning right on Golden Gate Rd., and following the signs that say "Camping." Yes, it's a campground, too. Also, trout ponds for fee fishing. Also, mobile homes and mobile-home sites for rent.

And don't forget the swimming. It has its own swimming pool, man-made, an acre in size, 10 feet deep, with water from clear-running Golden Gate Creek. And the tubing. In winter, besides skiing, they do a lot of tubing —sliding on big inflated inner tubes, cushioney, safer than toboggans. They do this on a special hill, separate from the ski hills but with its own rope tow, just like the two that serve the ski runs. The vertical rise, I'd say, is about 200 feet, although the owner's guess was more modest than that.

The scenery is more than catchy—one magnificent view that you catch before descending into the valley lets you see 10 miles or more to the southeast where this valley converges with the Minnesota River valley. The fall colors had faded when I drove in one day in late October, but it still was a grand sight.

The owners, Melvin and Carol Speckman, live in another farmhouse, south of the valley amid the rich, black fields of the upland. They own 400 acres in the valley and another 400 above.

The recreation area came into being happenstantially

—the way things happen with very industrious people. They had bought the valley to further a money-making hobby of Mrs. Speckman's—a duck and goose hatchery. Taking on custom hatching, making money. After about 10 years of that, they bought the valley farm for a breeding ground.

The hatchery grew into the biggest around. They were importing hatchable eggs from Holland and air-shipping them to China. Then, with market fluctuations, the whole thing got to be too much. They decided to get out of the hatchery business and go into recreation.

This was no cinch. They developed the swimming pool, the rental properties, the four trout ponds northwest of the campground, the Ping Pong and Foosball in the chalet recreation room, the skiing and tubing, the campsites with the electricity, sewer and water hook-ups, and the wilderness area across the creek for primitive camping (a lot of winter campers—snowmobilers—camp over there).

Yes, there's snowmobiling, too, in 300 acres of hills and valleys across the bridge. Some park their campers on the near side.

The recreation project started in 1970. Skiing started slowly, for most nearby residents were unfamiliar with it, but it's growing. Skiers are coming in from a 50-mile radius—Wabasso, Lamberton, Marshall, Wanda, Hector, Bird Island, New Ulm, Gibbon and other places,

The Golden Gate tubing hill gets a big play from youngsters and church groups who crave instant action without the learning process. They come in bunches of 75 or thereabouts. "One time we had 200," Speckman said.

BYWAYS

Trip No. 86 / Grandy

YOU COULD EASILY DRIVE through Grandy, Minn., a tiny town 5 miles north of Cambridge on Hwy. 65, without giving it any notice. However, if you like to browse among antiques and crafted things, that would be a mistake.

Grandy is devoted to almost nothing else. For instance, there is the Grandy Cabinet Shoppe, a young man's operation. Judd Johnson grew up on a farm near Grasston, 12 miles north, where a home remodeling do-it-yourself job got him started in cabinet and furniture making. He put up a new two-story block building on Grandy's main street (Hwy. 65) where, with other members of his family, he turns out tables, chairs, hutches, whatever you want, to your specifications.

Affiliated with the Cabinet Shoppe and also with Rocking Chair Antiques, at the other end of the street, is Jim Webster, a rangy former state patrolman and consummate artist at rosemaling.

Rosemaling is the old Norwegian art of painting colorful, scroll-like, floral designs on chests, plates, furniture, walls, beams or whatever you like.

After 13½ years with the State Patrol, Webster had quit to go into the manufacturing of snowmobile accessory parts, just before thaws and energy crunches struck. With the snowmobile business in the doldrums, Webster took rosemaling lessons.

It was the right move. Possessor of an unerring, rhy-

thmic hand, Webster began turning out objets d'art and selling them. Looking for an outlet, he bought an antique store in Grandy and later sold it. It is now Rocking Chair Antiques, where Webster still sells his work while collaborating with Judd Johnson in the Cabinet Shoppe.

Between the two is the Ceramic Coach studio, so named because it is housed in an old railroad coach. "Gifts," says the studio sign. Among them is a huge German wedding stein produced as an anniversary present. Finishes termed "graffiti," "sand-painting," and "dry brush" embellish the gifts. So do various stains, polishes, shading, translucencies.

*   *   *   *

Down the street, Rocking Chair Antiques occupies two buildings formerly used by Barney Spencer, who still maintains a collection in a building across the railroad tracks east of Hwy. 65. The Rocking Chair Antiques owner is Marjorie Srock. She moved here with her husband, Jack, a retired rancher, from the state of Washington in April, 1976. She and Jack hauled along her stock from an antique store she was running at Deer Park, northwest of Spokane. They've acquired a lot more at estate auctions since then.

They have an impressive collection that includes kerosene lamps, Depression glass, china, an old livery-stable clock, and an Edison wind-up cabinet phonograph that plays "The Snowy-Breasted Pearl," "Gypsy Love Song" and "I'll Take You Home Again, Kathleen."

At the south end of town is the Grandy Trading Post, specializing in taxidermy, sportsmen's gifts and antiques. It is in an antique, white-frame school building with belfry.

BYWAYS

Trip No. 87 / Northern to St. Francis to Crown

FOR A KICKY LITTLE AMBLE among the fens, thickets and farmland in northwestern Anoka and southwestern Isanti counties, start at Nowthen, Minn.

It's northwest of Anoka and northeast of Elk River. You can reach it from the latter by turning right across the tracks past George's Supermarket, crossing Hwy. 169,

and working your way north and east to where County Rds. 22, 63 and 5 come together.

That's Nowthen. Once it had a creamery, general store, post office, repair garage and auto and farm-implement dealership. It still has the latter. Economic attrition has reduced the creamery to foundation rocks, the general store to emptiness, baseball bleachers to a ghost's roost, and has left one family, the Greenbergs, pretty much in charge of downtown Nowthen.

Albin Greenberg, born on an Edina farm, started fixing tractors on his grandparent's farm, two miles north of Nowthen, when tractors were a new thing. The local farmers started buying tractors only when they found there was somebody around who could fix them—Albin.

254

He fixed them, started selling them, married Edith Skogquist, raised a family, took on an American Motors auto agency along with the implements and drew customers from five counties—still does.

Edith and Albin tell about how Nowthen got its name. The story is that James Hare, a Civil War veteran, the town's original postmaster and a bit of a character, was asked by the postal service to suggest a name (instead of a number) for his town. It was Hare's habit to begin his letters with "Now then . . ." and he preceded his list of suggested names the same way. The name pickers decided that "Nowthen" would be best.

From Nowthen ramble north on County Rd. 5 two miles to County Rd. 24 and followi ts curve line east into St. Francis past Al's Auto Salvage. "The Other Side" tavern, schools and churches (St. Patrick's Catholic, Trinity Lutheran, United Methodist, First Baptist), a weathered building labeled "Heritage House" and up to the Rum River Inn, an old building intelligently restructured with porch deck and riverview windows, overlooking the Rum just north of the bridge.

Inside, my wife and I had fresh hamburgers and met waitress Therese Meyenburg and co-owner Shashe Lepimski, of Lake George, two miles south. Last year she and Earl and Audrey Taylor bought the place.

The old inn, a stagecoach stop in the last century, had fallen on hard times when they bought it. It had a honky-tonk image, and the health authorities had closed it. The inn now has a dining room with newly cut view-commanding windows, live music in the evenings, an ambitious menu with vo-tech cooking graduates Paul Haas and Danny Baker in the kitchen, and a Rum River Multi-Trails Map for snowmobilers. Things are looking up.

From St. Francis go about four miles north on Hwy.

47, then about four miles west on Isanti County Rd. 8 to a sign pointing to the town of Crown a few blocks north.

Here on your right you'll find a delightful grocery, hardware and feed store run by Mabel Anderson, who bought it from her parents, Carl and Ella Hierlinger, in 1958.

She had a nice story about how Crown got its name. A pioneer had knelt by the trunk (or "crown") of a huge oak tree to measure it with his hands and, having done so, said, "We'll call this place Crown."

BYWAYS
Trip No. 88 / Stillwater Orchards

MID-OCTOBER IS THE time when dedicated apple-eaters drive out into the country to buy apples right at the source—the orchards.

It's the middle of the apple season, and the signs are out all over the growing regions in the hilly lake areas and up and down the river valleys.

Many connoisseurs, while biting a crisp one, like to admire the crimson and scarlet fruit, plump and smooth, decorating the rows of trees. But not many persons are aware of the progress in this branch of agriculture, especially in Minnesota.

Thor L. Aamodt, executive secretary of the Minnesota Fruit Growers association, summed it up for me very nicely while showing me around his handsome

Stillwater Orchards just north of Hwy. 36 west of Stillwater.

In one year Minnesota has produced 1 million bushels of apples. Because of the state's northerly latitude it's been a scientific struggle.

Over the past 20 years University of Minnesota horticulturists have developed a lot of apple-tree varieties that will survive Minnesota winters and produce durable fruit of excellent quality. Some of them are Fireside, Haralson, Minjon, Redwell and Regent. There also are mutations of these and others, still experimental and known by number.

While the foregoing apple names are quite familiar, it takes years before the various private orchards plant the trees, the trees grow up, and the fruit reaches the market in quantity. This is now happening.

Some of the greatest apple production advances are chemical. There are sprays now to control tree growth. When a tree reaches a size for convenient harvesting without climbing, spray it and it will stay that size and still produce heavily.

Another spray will eliminate 20 percent (or whatever percentage you wish, according to the mixture) of sprouting apples so the others won't be crowded.

Orchard soils are analyzed continuously so each year's fertilizing can be adjusted to meet the need.

Fruit production, says Aamodt, "has to be a highly scientific and somewhat technical procedure if one is to be successful. The great majority of apple growers throughout the country are now students of the subject."

Aamodt thought he was retiring to an apple orchard after 41 years of entomological work, most of them as state entomologist and University of Minnesota staff member.

Now during the harvest he hires 30 pickers and counts about 1,000 customers stopping on Saturdays and about 2,000 on Sundays.

BYWAYS

Trip No. 89 / Mellen, Wis.

THE NAME OF THE inventive genius who discovered it is lost to posterity, and the date when his discovery burst upon the tourist world like sunshine is similarly forgotten. But the whole thing must have happened somewhere in Wisconsin, for it is there that we find the full fruition of his intuitive thinking—distinctive, black and white markings for county roads—and signs with these markings on them to show you, at confusing corners and crossroads, which county road goes in which direction.

Some time thereafter some organizational genius (another nameless hero) got these same markings put on the maps which are distributed through filling stations—not all of them, but a great many. And now, today, using these maps, thousands of happy tourists, strangers to Wisconsin, are finding their way around Wisconsin's county roads happy in the security of knowing where they are going. At least a good share of the time.

Among the hundreds of curiously helpful county road markings in Wisconsin are some labeled "GG" which lead one from Clam Lake, Wis., to a town 20 miles northeast thereof, Mellen, Wis., which is something like 25 miles southeast of Ashland, Wis., which, as we all know, students, is an industrial settlement on the south shore of Lake Superior—Chequamegon Bay.

259

In "Chequamegon," incidentally, the accent is on the second syllable — "kwah!" These days on Chequamegon Bay there are white sails which, next to the Ashland coal docking facilities, likewise silhouetted against the blue water, make an interesting contrast.

However, to get back to "GG" from Clam Lake to Mellen: There are many hard maples along it, of the kind that may turn anything from lime gold, to pink, to crimson. And there are many bluish spruce spires and bushy longer-needled evergreens for contrast. The maples in mid-September were showing spots of color, sometimes startling.

This also was true of a drive northeast from Mellen along Hwy. 77 through Upson, Iron Belt, and Montreal to Hurley. Nevertheless, Mellen is a nice touring destination in itself.

Here in the increasingly beautiful verdure of second growth forest stand the tacky remnants and the lasting legacies of more profitable times, one of the latter being a masonry school building, bigger and grander than any building of its age that one would expect to find in these woods, and it is in use. The football team practices daily. Another is a fortress of a Victorian hotel, now labeled "Zaugg Nursing Home," facing the multi-track right of way just north of the Mellen depot.

In the park, near a statue of a charging World War I infantryman, beneath a willow tree, stands a plaque explaining that the tree sprang from another at the University of Wisconsin, which in turn was taken from a bush at Domremy, Haute Marne, France, the birthplace of Joan of Arc.

Through Mellen, near the center of town, runs the Bad River. At this point, between the railroad tracks and the bridge, with the big school some distance in the background, an unpretentious house of rare patina stands beside the river. A retired blacksmith, and wife lived here.

"We moved here when the river flooded and took our other house in 1946," she said. "We want to get a better one."

From where I stood I couldn't imagine a better one.

CHAPTER XV   ANTIQUITY

Trip No. 90 / Money Creek

THE MINUTE A READER told me about the village of Money Creek I wanted to go, but I waited because I knew how appealing that section of the state can be when the green begins to deepen on the hillsides and glow in the willows, poplars and elms.

I wasn't disappointed. Along the Mississippi on the way down the riverbank cedars seemed thicker and darker and the sandstone outcroppings even looked fresher and yellower. And here and there among the upper twigs of the tall trees I could see that pale green glow.

I took Hwy. 43 seven miles southwest from Winona, then left on Hwy. 76, then 13 miles southeast and south into Money Creek. On 43 you climb through a wide valley. On 76, after a stretch on the flat, you descend into another valley.

The soil is rich in the valley. You'll see some handsome barns. Corn and milk are the primary products. Halfway down the hill I noticed an enviable place on the right with white buildings, green grass, and two earth dams where the creek was backed up into fish ponds, one behind the other, like steps.

Two little creeks join just northwest of where the highway bridges their combined flow. This you follow downstream toward the Root River for about two miles. Here a sign, "Money Creek," points to the left.

I took a swing around the town (it doesn't take long). I saw an old stone church with a big stained glass window. It was inscribed "Methodist Episcopal," and a corner stone, evidently commemorating a prior building, bore the dates 1857-1909.

Then I stopped at a little old green building that looked like a store. I found it was vacant, however, and this led to the further discovery that the town's sole commercial establishment was Ledebuhr's Garage and Filling Station.

As I pulled in, Leroy Ledebuhr, who was running the station for his father, August, was walking home across the street to get his lunch. He was brought up there, he said, went through Money Creek Grade School and then took the bus to high school in Houston, five miles to the south.

He sent me to see his grandparents, Mr. and Mrs. Paul Ledebuhr, in the house just the other side of the garage.

His grandmother spent her girlhood in the valley. "We'd slide on these hills," she said. "My brother skated on the millpond and every pond he could find."

Leroy's grandfather said he built the mill house by the millpond. "It's used as a barn now. No millpond there any more. The dam went out.

"There used to be twice as many people in town as there are now. Two stores. Now they're both closed. It took more people to run things in those days. People had lots of children. Later on they stopped having big families. Didn't have any use for them."

His wife laughed. "What a saying!"

"Well, it's true. Today it takes a piece of land the size of three farms to support one of those big tractors."

When I asked how Money Creek got its name, he

said he didn't put any stock in the story everybody told, but his wife told it anyway:

"When the pioneers came here looking for claims, some of them camped by the creek. One of them lost his wallet with all his money in it. After hunting for it and not finding it, they always called the place 'Money Creek'."

"There's another Money Creek, not a town but a creek, around Pilot Mound and St. Charles," her husband said. "They used to call this town Clinton, but there was another Clinton, so the post office had to be named something else. So they started calling it after the creek."

Feeling confusion coming on, I took my leave. I returned to Winona via Winona County Road 17 running north out of Witoka. This way was shorter but equally pretty.

ANTIQUITY
Trip No. 91 / Ghost Country

CARL H. SOMMER was president of the Rush City, Minn., State Bank for many years.

"I have a trip suggestion to make to you," he wrote. "One sees and hears about western ghost cities, but never a ghost 'country.'

". . . I was born three miles west of Rush City Oct. 23, 1877. Being the oldest living person born in this vicinity, I have always been interested in early events and can remember instances since I was 3½ years old . . ."

He went on to explain how the St. Croix River basin, is "mostly heavy soil and hardwood timber" while the Wisconsin side is "sand and jack pines" in this latitude 75 miles northeast of Minneapolis.

This sandy soil wouldn't support good crops, but "in the later 1800s and early 1900s," he wrote, "some landman got people from Sweden to settle" there, where the nice green pines reminded them of home and there was plenty of timber for cabin building.

This is the area which, to Sommer, is ghost country.

From his early teens through young manhood it was full of congenial people struggling to make a go of it.

It might not have been good farming country, but to young Sommer it was a happy paradise. The streams had trout. There were ducks and grouse in the meadows. Even forest fires left a bonus—burgeoning blueberries, ripe and full, after the trees were gone and the sun came in. Time and again he crossed on the ferry with horse and buggy.

Gradually, however, the immigrants left "the barrens," as the sandy region became known, for better land elsewhere. Meanwhile, Sommer, having got a job at the bank at 15, went on to become its president, marry, raise a family and eventually get a plaque for being one of four bankers in the United States with 75 years in the banking field.

The governor cited his lifetime of service in business, civic and church affairs.

When I met him in 1968, Sommer had slowed down a bit. He walked with a cane and had somebody take care of the backyard gladiolus garden where he hybridized some orchid gladioli. He had a bit of asthma. ("My doctor says I could clear it up if I'd stop smoking these cigars, but he says at my age he won't tell me to quit.")

None of this, however, prevented him from meeting people at his favorite eating place, the Grant House on Hwy. 61 in Rush City. I had lunch with him there (chicken, peas, potatoes, blueberry pie), and he guided me across the St. Croix (Hwy. 70 bridge) and through the barrens.

He pointed out the wire grass, once harvested for carpeting, the abandoned railroad grade, the house to which he walked nine miles when he got stuck, the confluence of Trade River and Cowan Creek, up which kidnappers once took Theodore Hamm ("I might easily have stumbled upon them because I often fished there.")

He told how the village of Sunrise was built across the river in anticipation of a railroad that never came and how the founder of the Rush City Post tied a cow to the tracks to make the "through" train stop.

He handed me an account of the early days written by a Mrs. W. W. Lee, who would be 125 if she were alive today.

Once in a blizzard she waited long hours at the window of their 10 by 15 cabin (Lee had brought lumber for a bigger house) until "at last I heard the rattling of chains . . . he had to leave the load behind and had followed the oxen home, wallowing through the drifts."

Husband and wife often had to go on separate missions with sled and oxen. Once, with the children, she had to dip enough wheat out of 120-pound sacks so that the oxen could pull the sled out of a rotten log where it had stuck. Then she returned the wheat to the sacks.

Again, "one day as I was driving along the bluff a large wolf came out and began jumping at the buggy wheel . . . (and) at the horse's flanks . . . I kept beating him (with a buggy whip) and at last he gave up . . ."

One day in May "we decided we had to go to Rush City to get the remainder of our goods. We left the little girls, 9 and 3, at home in the shack, expecting to return before dark. On the trip back I held our clock in my lap . . . the wagon lurched . . . . It was an eight-day clock and there was no stopping it, so it struck repeatedly . . . .

"When we reached the river there was a log drive coming down. Have you ever seen one? The logs were so close together that you couldn't see the water . . . . Many a log driver lost his life by being careless when he walked across the logs . . . . Mr. Deering brought some hay for our oxen.

"Working his way in a small bateaux, he took us back to the ferry house. That was a terrible night. I walked the floor all night watching the river thinking of my little girls alone at the shack. But the river cleared in the morning—the Wannigan went by, and we got our team across and home and found the children safe.

"The baby hadn't been frightened, as she had perfect confidence in her sister, who knew how to light a candle, prepare food and keep the fire going. Our children had to be very self-reliant."

Of course, there were floods, too. In fact, "I could go on for hours relating experiences, some funny, many sad. Scarlet fever, typhoid, diphtheria, etc. On nice summer evenings we often took our picnic supper down into one of those shady glens under some of the most magnificent pines I've ever seen . . . . Other times we went trout fishing at a brook, or hitched up our team and wagon to go hazel nutting in the fall . . . .

"Now we had five children and we knew it was pointless to stay there any longer . . . . the Swedish neighbors were all leaving for better farm land. . . . Mr. Lee had purchased 40 acres . . . south of Rush City. We took down our barn and best buildings and hauled them to this new location."

Carl Sommer's eyes lit up when he recalled the busy days and the hunting and fishing around the barrens. It's nearly all treed over now, but he could still find his way and point out some of his favorite spots, where he caught fish or the blue-berrying was good.

ANTIQUITY

Trip No. 92 / Franconia

THE WEATHERED SIDING on one or two of the houses
in the little settlement on the Minnesota side of the St.
Croix River suggests that they have been standing here
since long ago.

They have, indeed. Others have rotted into the
ground or been swept away by the water.

In these days of the swollen river, it's easier to
imagine the trials and hardships of early Franconia than
in drier years.

You'll find the place downstream from Taylors Falls.
There is no sign at the turn-off. It leaves Hwy. 95 eastward about one-quarter-mile south of its junction with
Hwy. 8. There is a white sign for a tree nursery and
flower garden on the westward arm of the little inter-
secting road.

Turning east, one descends through the greenery
down a long winding hill. Eight or nine on a bobsled,
children once shot around these curves.

At the bottom before crossing little Lawrence Creek
(no sign), you'll go under high elm branches. To the
left is a trunk sprouting out of a long roof. A breezeway
was built around the tree.

Across the creek I found "Vitalis" and a boat rental
sign in front of a new rambler. The name is older than
the house. The boat renter is Adolph Vitalis. His father,
Elof, built the bobsleds.

270

The fishing was good but not boat rentals, Adolph told me. It was a cold spring.

I drove to the river, where you can park and launch a canoe. Through weeds and undergrowth, about 150 feet upstream, one can find the stone foundations of a sawmill. Its last owner was Adolph's grandfather.

"In the old days," said Adolph, "before they had a cemetery down here, they'd bury a man where he fell. They just dug a hole and buried him and said a few words.

"Later when they got the cemetery they didn't have anybody to start it with. There was one Irishman, so they shot him to start the cemetery."

At least, he admitted with a smile, that's what he tells the Irishmen. Vitalis is a Swedish name.

The "old days" were the days of Franconia, a lumber town that took many a beating from floods along the riverbank.

Its buildings are gone. Where the post office stood is

271

a modest granite monument flanked by arborvitae: "Franconia . . . settled in 1852 . . . Franconia Old Settlers Association."

In a yellow house half a block up the street from Adolph's lives his sister, Mrs. Arthur Swanlund. She was secretary-treasurer of the Old Settlers for a few years and might be persuaded for 50 cents to part with a copy of the group's Franconia history, with photographs.

ANTIQUITY

Trip No. 93 / Minnesota River Valley

A GOOD COMBINATION OF autumn foliage and Minnesota history is available at several points along the Minnesota River.

One of the many interesting tours in this area starts at Granite Falls, a town well worth detailed examination if you belong to the "this certainly has its points" school of thought whose members dream of living in towns like Granite Falls some day. I happen to be president.

Just notice some of the neighborhoods and their views. History enters the picture as you head southeast on highway 67, which crosses the Yellow Medicine river. A highway plaque has this to say:

"In 1854 the agency for the Sioux Indians was established near the Yellow Medicine River about a mile from its mouth (where it joins the Minnesota). During the Sioux outbreak in August 1862 many whites from this agency and nearby missions were escorted to safety by friendly Indians."

Five miles farther along the road is a crossroad with the Rockvalley store on one corner and the Rockvalley Lutheran church on another. Here a sign points west to "Historic Plaque," and if you drive west 7/10 of a mile on this country road, you find a grassy, cemetery-like plot with "Sioux Indian War" over the gate and a memorial shaft inside.

The plaque is headed "Battle of Wood Lake" and explains that "near this point on Sept. 23, 1862, during the Sioux outbreak, Little Crow's warriors ambushed General Sibley's troops . . . The Indians were defeated with white losses of 41 killed and wounded." In point of fact, the monument explains if you go inside, seven were killed and 34 were wounded.

Back on 67 continue south to highway 19 and turn left to Redwood Falls. Here is one of the most scenic parks in southern Minnesota. It was Alexander Ramsey State Park until growing Redwood Falls enveloped it and it was turned over to the city.

The Redwood River, a Minnesota River tributary which runs through the park, rushes around among some rocks in a steep descent and then drops about 50 feet into a shady gorge which poses quite a problem for photographers, I can tell you, when the sun is shining up above.

Besides the grandeur of its big trees and steep valley terrain this park offers picnic grounds and a small zoo among whose inhabitants you will notice a pair of American bison and their offspring. This trio appears quite domestic as it feeds on hay.

Also present are a raccoon, a bear and a white-side-walled Canadian honker which sounds better than most modern automobiles.

Another six miles along highway 19 will take you to Morton. If you take a short jaunt north on highway 71 here, you'll find a sign directing you westward to Birch Coulee Memorial park and more history.

It's a small park but worth a turn down the hill through its woodsy valley. On the grassy plain above are some markers, monuments and a plaque telling how 160 troops were attacked by Sioux at dawn Sept. 2, 1862, "half a mile east of this point" and the fight lasted 30 hours.

Farther east along highway 19, between Morton and Franklin, is the Redwood ferry historic plaque. The parking spot offers a nice view of the valley which is especially pretty when the leaves turn.

"At the old ferry landing below this point on Aug. 18, 1862," says the plaque, "Capt. John Marsh, an interpreter and 46 men . . . were ambushed by Sioux Indians. The interpreter and 24 men were killed and Capt. Marsh was drowned while trying to escape. The site is marked . . . ."

There is no marked trail to the site and finding it is something of a project, but if one had time and rubber boots, it might be worth trying.

ANTIQUITY
Trip No. 94 / Winnebago Indian Agency

SOMEBODY WROTE IN, so long ago that I've forgotten who or when, to tell me that there might be something of interest down around the old Winnebago Indian Agency at St. Clair, Minn.

I just got around to it and I'm glad I did.

One reason, outside of the pretty drive down Hwy. 169 to Mankato, is that I met Clay Boswell. He is an interesting and engaging source of historical information.

A spare and wiry 77, he was helping with the farming and climbing telephone poles to wire the barnyard.

"A fellow came in and said, 'You shouldn't be up there. You're too old for that.' I asked him how old he thought I was, and he said, 'Why, you must be nearly 65.' " Height never did bother him, Boswell told me.

Every year a friend takes him fox-hunting in an airplane. He watches the ground as they go skimming along and never gets sick.

Boswell's grandparents on both sides of his family came into the St. Clair area shortly after the Winnebago agency was established in 1855.

Boswell took me to the old agency house, 1.7 miles east of the center of town. He showed me where the timbers were cut and milled from walnut trees by the LeSueur River and where the bricks were kilned.

Mervin L. Preston and family had lived in the old agency house for the past seven years. He was farming the land around it back to the river. Five Preston boys, including a set of twins, were running around where the Winnebagos walked.

After the New Ulm battle with the Sioux (1862) the United States Cavalry herded the white settlers around St. Clair into Tivoli, a small settlement three miles to the northwest. Sioux scouts killed one of their cavalry guards. Said Boswell:

"He was watering the horses in the river when he saw the Sioux in the weeds. He might have lived except that he put up a holler. The Sioux shot him. My grandmother saw him die on the doorstep of a little log cabin by the bridge. He is buried in Tivoli Cemetery.

"The Sioux tried to get the Winnebagos to join the uprising and help them mop up the whites, but Chief Decoria of the Winnebagos had too many white friends. He wouldn't help.

"Some of the white settlers saw how good the land was and talked the government higher ups into moving the Winnebagos out. This was started before the Sioux uprising. The Winnebagos who had a little shack and had settled down weren't bothered. They took title to their land just like anybody else. Some of them made good farmers. They were nice people."

In Boswell's school about a quarter of the children were part or all Winnebago. Eventually, however, all the known Winnebagos scattered. He blames the government dole. "They were always looking ahead to the next check."

Sumner Tillotson, who built Boswell's grandfather's house (still standing) had a Winnebago wife. They left after selling the house, and Boswell doesn't know what became of them.

Boswell kept flocks of wild geese and wood ducks—fed and made pets of them.

"Do you eat them?" I asked.

He laughed. "I've never killed a single one."

ANTIQUITY

Trip No. 95 / Ottawa, Minn.

I AM REPORTING HEREWITH a trip which interested me but which I will have to recommend with reservations.

I had never heard of Ottawa, Minn., until I got a letter from Albert Shelley of Madelia:

"Ottawa was a town even before Le Sueur was started. Once had a post office, hotel, several stores, depot and brick yard. All gone except a few old timers . . ."

I found Ottawa by taking Hwy. 112 south from Le Sueur and turning west on a surfaced country road where the highway itself takes a right-angle turn to the east.

There aren't any signs saying "Ottawa," but you'll know you're there when you begin to notice some of the town's hollow-eyed, deserted architecture, squarely and solidly constructed of beautifully textured rough, tan native stone, much of its warmly colored surfaces enhanced by the contrast of standing and climbing greenery.

To those who share my susceptibility to the romance and allure of desuetude and decay I can recommend these happily neglected relics freely.

To the rest I can recommend certain other visually engaging aspects of the locality but not without including certain cautionary notes. The first of these will have to be of an olfactory nature.

As you drive around you will notice here and there among the trees some long corrugated steel shelters. They shelter a considerable number of cages, and in the cages are minks. Minks are meat eaters. You might not want to linger around these mink farms as you would around the Lake Harriet Rose Gardens.

Seeking a view of the Minnesota River (hidden by the trees), I drove around town and admired some of the well-kept and lived-in houses of the same native stone as the deserted ones. Noticing the span between inside and outside doors on one, I guessed the wall's thickness at about a foot and a half.

Driving closer to the river, I pulled into a yard where four friendly brothers and their friendly collie came out to greet me. They were the sons of Mr. and Mrs. Maxie E. Bennett.

They showed me a broken clay wine bottle (cemented together by their mother) which they had uncovered by some of the old town ruins in the woods and readily agreed to show me through the woods to the river, where they sometimes get catfish.

We went by some fences made of old mink cages and were upon the riverbank much sooner than I had expected. I had imagined that we were on a bluff. I was surprised to find that we were near water level. I remembered that I had heard there was a ferry crossing at Ottawa in the days of the Sioux Indians.

Before leaving I called at the farm of Edward H. and Merrill P. Loose and their sister, Mrs. Minnie Dressel, all residents of long standing. They recalled when the town had a depot, an elevator, a creamery, a blacksmith shop, a saloon, a store, a post office, two churches (Methodist and Catholic) and a school. It has none of these now.

But it does have a silica sand open pit mine and plant, down the road a piece, from which the white sand is shipped out to glass factories. This has replaced the old stone quarries as the mink farms have supplanted trapping.

ANTIQUITY

Trip No. 96 / Hutchinson

THERE ARE THE MODERN museums, neatly cateorgized and sharply, clearly put into context via audio-visual tapes and guides. Then there are the old ones where things have accumulated, cataloged after a fashion, departmentalized where possible, worked in where space permits, but all there for you to search and discover.

It's in these museums that nostalgia sometimes can sneak up and stop you dead.

It happened in Hutchinson at the McLeod County Historical Museum (corner of 1st Av. and Jefferson St.) in the company of curator Bertha Steinke, a widow and grandmother who has done a lot of the cataloguing and inventorying single-handed.

"I'm 84," she had said, "but I come from good stock."

We were walking down a hall in the 2½-story Victorian house-museum, built in 1902 for $10,000 by Frank Brabec, a department store owner. Two mementos hung framed on the wall—one a wedding picture and vows surrounded by finely fashioned rosettes of multi-colored wool yarn. The other was a son's confirmation record

280

signalized by a colored, sagging, serpentine candle. The reds, blues and greens held fresh in the wool. Time had faded the warped candle. I looked from one to the other, assessing the bygone work that went into them, dealing with the specifics of nostalgia.

"It kind of gets you."

"Yes," she agreed.

Mrs. Steinke opened a closet door. There it stood staring at me. A mummy. Height: about 5 feet, Face: wide. Expression: faintly amused. Condition: shriveled.

"Where did this come from?"

"A carnival woman," she said. "She spent some time in Hutchinson and turned it over to the Historical Society.

Said it was Peruvian. It went into the library, then the high school, then the museum basement, and I had it put in here, An exchange student from Peru looked at it and said, 'Yes, that's the way they looked.' She said there was an Indian tribe in Peru with unusually big heads for the size of their bodies."

I learned where Hutchinson got its name. In a corner stands a small portable organ, which some of the singing New England Hutchinsons, who settled Hutchinson, Minn., carried on tour.

Three singing Hutchinsons, brothers Asa, John and Judson(called on New Englander W. W. Pendergast in his Milwaukee photographic studio in 1855. They were heading for Kansas. Pendergast persuaded them to veer off to the northwest. He praised the scenery. They traveled from St. Anthony to Shakopee to Glencoe and settled on the Crow River site where Hutchinson stands, The New Englanders started it. There was a lot of music and religion mixed up in it. And temperance.

"At one time," Mrs. Steinke said, "the rule was that if intoxicating beverages were found in your house, you forfeited the house."

But there was no rule against singing. The Hutchinson family members were singers. They traveled a lot. An old four-foot poster proclaims:

"The Young Folks Are Coming. The Hutchinson Family, Tribe of Asa . . . [have] given more concerts and appeared before more people than any other American musical organization . . . . Art, harmony, mirth and sentiment. Songs of home, hope and happiness . . . melts the audience , . . carries them away on a tidal wave . . . ."

The Tribe of Asa has departed, but Hutchinsonians played their parts for the Bicentennial. Sharon Cogley was Abby Hutchinson, who toured with her brothers.

Barney Schendler was Asa. Jeff Bentz was John. Al Huff was Judson.

An aged pamphlet titled "20th Century Song Book" (1904) lay on a casetop. I turned to "Rock Me to Sleep, Mother."

" Backward, turn backward, O time in thy flight . . . . Make me a child again just for tonight . . . . Mother, come back from your echoless shore—Take me again to your heart as of yore . . . ."

Every other page in the "20th Century Song Book" carries a patent medicine ad.

The one opposite "Rock Me to Sleep, Mother"—"I suffered 12 years with menorrhagia, My advice to suffering women—take Wine of Cardui."

The museum hours are 2-4 p.m. Wednesdays and Sundays. If you want to arrange a special tour, contact Mrs. Steinke, 209 Hassan St., Hutchinson, Minn. 55350.

CHAPTER XVI   AUTUMN

Trip No. 97 / Grand Rapids to Big Fork

GRAND RAPIDS, MINN., the home of the Blandin Paper Mill and a community with a certain residential elegance about it, is a pretty place to visit in late September or early October.

Hard maples mixed with the evergreens here and there offer some startling flashes of color. These things change so fast, but some golden aspen leaves with some light coming through them were as dazzling as any I've seen.

I don't know of many rides to match the one from Grand Rapids up Hwy. 38 to Bigfork and Scenic State Park, a park which I hadn't seen before and which, for its big pines on Sandwick Lake, must rank among the state's most beautiful.

Heading north on 38 just five miles from the middle of town, you really should stop for a gander at Daniel M. Gunn Memorial Park, established and maintained by the Blandin Foundation.

Grand Rapids friends told me to "turn left at the pink store" 11 miles north of town for a drive along Deer Lake. Good advice. The flourishing verdure bulged along both sides and sometimes met overhead. Keep to the right and you'll wind up back on 38. You don't see much of the lake, but one brief opening in the trees affords a long view, for you're up rather high.

Back on 38 drive 8.3 miles to the Continental Divide. If you watch to the right beyond the divide you'll notice a high TV relay tower and near it a rangers' tower. If you like to climb tall ladders, here's one for you. "You may climb the tower if you wish," says the sign, but the United States Department of Agriculture forestry service "cannot assume any liability." Neither can I.

Bigfork, 45 miles north of Grand Rapids, has a lumber mill which is remarkably productive—the Kajala Lumber Co. mill. Sawing has stopped for this year, but you might like to take a look at the mill, anyway. It's just a couple of blocks west of the main street, on the Bigfork River.

The sawmill is in a big weathered old building. Some of the equipment in it is new. Some of it's been there since the turn of the century. Kenneth R. Nelson, a filer (he sharpens the teeth on the huge saws), told me how the logs are piled up on the river ice until it melts and then are washed in the river and hoisted into the mill's second story on an endless chain.

He showed me where the pond or deck man, the sawyer, the tail sawyer, the edgeman, the resaw man, the trimmer man and the grader all stand. There's a little platform from which the public can watch when the mill is going. It usually starts around February. The best time to watch is in April when the white pines are going through, Nelson said.

Itasca County Road 7 will take you to Scenic State Park, seven miles east of town. It's a dandy—boats, sandy beach, fishing and hiking. There are cabins and camp sites. I wouldn't mind staying in one some time.

AUTUMN

Trip No. 98 / Lutsen to Jay Cooke Park

IN LATE OCTOBER PEOPLE ARE still vacationing along the North Shore of Lake Superior—not hunters or fishermen, just idle vacationers.

The fall colors are past their peak and the trees have lost their leaves in many areas, but some people find this twiggy bleakness appealing, especially when the big waves come pounding in, and I can understand this.

At Lutsen, Minn., 90 miles up the shore from Duluth, Minn., you'll find quite a variety of groups, and ages, relaxing in the lounge, walking the shore, or taking some of the hiking trails up the Poplar River, across which the Nelsons, owners of the Lutsen resort, have built a charming covered bridge for pedestrians.

If you go as far as Lutsen, go another 20 miles and take a look at Grand Marais, Minn., where the Gunflint Trail heads into the wilderness.

If you do, it is worth remembering that this village is the summer home of a painters' art colony. And to understand that, drive through town and out to the lakeshore U.S. Coast Guard station. Notice the picturesque fishing shacks along the way and, when you get out by the breakwater, turn around and look across the glistening bay at the town against its big hill backdrop, the biggest hill being known as "Sawtooth."

Unsurprisingly, you will notice new motel and hotel
development around town. Howard Joynes, manager
of the Ben Franklin store, says the overnight capacity
is now about 500.

Back in Duluth the Skyline Pkwy. ("30 miles of
scenic driving 700 feet above lake level") is at its best
in the sunshine, but for a bonus thrill, try it at dusk when

the sky is fading to purple and the lights are going on.

You might have seen Jay Cooke State Park along the St. Louis River just west of Duluth many times, but if you haven't seen it at this time of year, you'll see more of it than before. That's simply because the leaves are off most of the trees, and you can see through the branches. You get much longer views that way.

The hard sharp-edged rocks, around which the St. Louis River boils and rushes, were sea-bottom sediment two billion years ago. They were compacted into shale and then into slate. Eventually deep movements in the earth's crust fractured and tilted them.

Driving southeast through Jay Cooke Park from Carlton, Minn., you come out on Hwy. 23. There to the right or southwest you'll see the Mont du Lac ski area.

Turning the other way, northeast, on Hwy. 23, you'll come to the Old Depot Inn, once a depot serving the Lake Superior and Mississippi Railroad (1870), later the St. Paul and Duluth and Northern Pacific railroads, and now a recommendable restaurant.

AUTUMN

Trip No. 99 / Wabasha

"I CAME DOWNSTAIRS AND, my God, it was black with cars all the way down to the river. I went out in the kitchen, and I said, 'God, there's been a terrible accident!' "

"They said, 'Accident, my eye. Those are people waiting for dinner.'

"We fed 700 that day. I was back in the kitchen making pies and cakes—got my aunt out of retirement and she started making dough. We cooked all afternoon and kept asking, 'Are there still people in the lobby?'

"The answer was 'Yes.'"

The place: Wabasha's Anderson House. The time: two decades ago, the day after "The Fruit of a Family Tree—Country Cooking" by Evelyn Burke appeared in the *Minneapolis Tribune*.

The speaker: Jeanne McCaffrey Hall, recalling the the past as she worked behind the desk in the lobby of the same Anderson House.

Walk in and she'll give you a friendly greeting.

Old hotels, like people, have their ups and downs. The Anderson House is having an up, but it's gone both ways.

Mrs. Hall's grandmother, Ida Anderson, 24 years younger than her husband, William, gave the hotel its first real "up" when she bought it in 1902 and opened a kitchen and dining room.

Until then it had been just an inn—no meals—dating to 1856 and called The Hurd House.

Ida Anderson brought the hotel her enthusiasm and Dutch cooking from Pennsylvania. It prospered, and two of her daughters, one of them Jeanne McCaffrey Hall's mother Verna, continued the success for many years.

Vegetable salads, chicken dumplings, rolls, a dozen kinds of bread, "double-Dutch fudge pie," an endless variety of entrees and goodies brought in the customers. Jeanne and other members of the family helped.

Time passed, and the two daughters of Ida were pushing 80. They decided to sell the hotel.

"Gee, we were stupid," Jeanne says today. "No sooner was it sold than we regretted it. We'd walk by and see the change. It had been run with so much warmth and personal interest.

"The buyer was rather an introverted man. He was divorced, the dining room was closed. Then it reopened for 18 months with women from outside running it. One of them shot and killed her lover—pretty heavy stuff for Wabasha. The dining room closed again."

Eleven years went by before Ida Anderson's descendants got her hotel back. Jeanne's son John, once the hotel was repurchased, moved back to the hotel from a successful kitchen operation at Rochester's Ramada Inn, and other family members rallied round his mother.

That was in July 1976, and things are hopping again.

"Boy, I'm telling you, we really had to move," Jeanne said. "We couldn't afford to be closed very long. We carpeted the dining room, did the room over, did the lobby, put in Ida's Ice Cream Parlor and then when we were tiling the kitchen, the floor fell in under us.

"For awhile it was one step forward and five backward. My mother (Verna) is very religious. She went through 20 rosaries while we were trying to get this place open, really frightened that there was too much to be done."

They did it. They put different wallpaper in every room. Some Rubenesque nudes on the wallpaper in the men's room occasioned some hesitation. Tourists have been snapping pictures of this and other wallpaper and furnishings. They also have been buying antique furniture right out of the rooms.

AUTUMN

Trip No. 100 / North or South

NORTH OR SOUTH, either direction can stir the scenery lover in the fall of the year.

Question: What is as exciting as the waves pounding into the rockbound Lake Superior North Shore in a 20-mile-an-hour wind?

Answer: Looking down on the Mississippi from the precipitous edge of Buena Vista Park at Alma, Wis., on a calm sunny day with the gulls spreading their wings and cutting white silhouettes against the dark river far below you.

The city of Alma, which maintains Buena Vista Park high on the bluff above it, has one picnic table on a promontory where one almost feels he is sitting in the sky.

Across the river and upstream the admirers of Lake City, Minn., are riding high with the Lake City waterfront project, a boaters' mecca and barge fishermen's delight.

The large parking area is generous enough for large numbers of visitors, and there is a big fishing barge with lamplights away from the breakwater. The trailer court is equipped with utilities. The 400-boat marina is neat as a parade line.

Lake City runs the place as a project of long-proven attractiveness. The Chicago Queen excursion boat is privately run, but the rest is municipal.

The trailer park has electricity, city water and city sewers. The city rents out the trailer spaces and boat slips, and a bathhouse serves a bathing beach on the project's northeast edge.

The improvements cost nearly $500,000, but rental and service charges are paying off the debt.

*   *   *   *

Along the North Shore of Lake Superior one finds, if the wind is blowing, a lot of wild waves dashing on the rocks at Tofte, where motel windows are high but not so high that the spray can't reach them.

The road back to the ski area at Lutsen is at its most picturesque in the fall. Farther up the shore, past Grand Marais, we have the Grand Portage National Monument, where the North West Company Post (first built around 1778 and abandoned in 1803) is being reconstructed.

Take the tour within the palisade guided by leaflets available at the gate.

The palisade, rebuilt near the lake where ruins were found, enclosed warehouses and quarters where trade goods arrived by canoe from the east and tons of furs portaged from northern outposts were checked and loaded for Montreal.